CIO 2.0
Stories From the Frontline #1

CIO Community

WRITING MATTERS PUBLISHING

CIO 2.0: CIO Stories From The Frontline #1

First published in April 2018

Writing Matters Publishing (UK)
info@writingmatterspublishing.com
www.writingmatterspublishing.com

ISBN 978-1-9999187-3-6 (pbk)

Editor: Pat Lynes, Christian McMahon and Andrew Priestley.

Contributors: Christian McMahon, David Knowles, Steve Homan, Chris Lord, James Mottram, Tony Walters, Peter Blower, Kevin Robins, Ken Towning, Paul Hobbs, Malcolm Lambell, Chris Michael, Yiannis Levantis, Heena Prajapat, Pat Lynes, Abby Ewen.

Contents

What mark are you going to leave on the world?

Christian McMahon and Pat Lynes thought it would be a good project to collate a series of stories from CIOs and turn it into a book for the CIO/CTO/CDO community. Incredibly, in just three months from the time of inception, this became a reality, with the book becoming an Amazon #1 best seller.

Big thanks to all co-authors for sharing your thoughts and experiences:

David Knowles, Steve Homan, Chris Lord, James Mottram, Tony Walters, Peter Blower, Kevin Robins, Ken Towning, Paul Hobbs, Malcolm Lambell, Chris Michael, Yiannis Levantis, Heena Prajapat and Abby Ewen.

It was a great experience and we all hope you enjoy the thought leadership, value and insight this book provides.

Our royalties will be going to the *Institute of Cancer Research* and *S&S* will be making an extra donation to help where it is needed.

So if you could please help support this by buying a copy, it would be much appreciated.

Through this initiative *S&S* are the first organisation to carry a *supportmark* which represents our commitment to deliver social impact.

Are you are a business owner offering a product or service? Are interested in generating investment that goes towards social impact? Join us and carry a *supportmark*. We believe we are stronger together.

What mark are you going to leave on the world?

To the power of crowdsourcing.

Introduction

The CIO and the CIO role has never been under so much pressure. It feels like we are at a tipping point within the business at large, where huge transformation needs to happen for most organisations just to stay in the game.

As 20th Century business models collide with the pace of change in the 21st Century, an opportunity exists for the CIO to bring their wealth of experience and unique position to take a variety of different routes to facilitate this seismic business transformation that is happening around us.

We have both met thousands of CIOs who we talk to about their career, changing needs, desires and what they want for themselves in the next decade. Many talk about wanting to move away from the permanent CIO circuit and start to move beyond the CIO role into COO or even CEO; and others want to start developing a portfolio journey for themselves.

We live in a world now where there is an abundance of opportunities for CIOs to start developing a journey into how they use their experience, IP, know-how and style on a gig-by-gig basis.

Sullivan & Stanley was created to be at the heart of this executive and knowledge gig economy and we attract numerous opportunities for CIOs for fractional, CIO as a service type work, interim work, NED connections, trusteeships and CIO-in-residence opportunities to partner with Private Equity firms.

On the back of the market shift we were seeing, and the series of conversations both Christian and I were having with the CIO community, we decided to set up a non-vendor, non-salesy CIO community creating a safe environment and support network for those looking to evolve their skills, influence, network and make the jump into the next decade.

CIO 2.0 was born. It is a movement of business leaders with a technology focus.

We formed CIO 2.0 as a means for CIOs to network and help each other without the vendor agenda.

There was nothing really available as a *support* network for CIOs and our group has provided an environment which has encouraged collaboration through a social network and a number of focused/social events where we meet in group workshops and produce practical output.

The community acts as an open support network for CIOs for what is typically an isolated position. It is also a think-tank and knowledge sharing movement to help CIOs on their journey into the next decade. Whether that is more of a career journey into COO/CEO, or becoming a Portfolio CIO, Advisory CIO, Investor CIO, Social CIO, Start-up CIO and/or other portfolio activities with how they want to work, advise, create and lead.

The community fuses both an online experience via a social network, and an offline experience via CIO workshops. We have workshopped many themes including launching a portfolio career, hitting a new gig with impact and of course, where this book comes in, branding yourself as an executive and sharing your IP via content.

Welcome to *CIO 2.0 – Stories From The Frontline #1*.

In advance of one of these events regarding how to improve the personal brand of CIOs within the group, the idea for a crowdsourced book was hatched. We invited business coach, author and publisher, Andrew Priestley to an event to talk about how he has crowdsourced and curated books for others. At the end of his session we raised the opportunity of creating a book for our group.

Any initial feelings of nervousness about becoming an author were quickly replaced by excitement with 16 CIOs quick to take up the opportunity to get involved in this book.

We have worked with the authors throughout the creation process, as although they are exceptionally skilled in their craft, writing a chapter for a book was new to many.

What they have created has been amazing and every chapter in this book gives you something to contemplate. Each chapter gives you the insight in to what it takes to be a CIO and the plethora of issues and challenges that the role faces every day.

This book is a testament to some of the exceptional work that many CIOs have done and hopefully these real-world solutions will inspire and help many in the role or those taking the next step in their careers.

There is nothing like real world examples to help you through a situation and realise that others have been there before you and faced the same problem, achieving a successful outcome.

The take-up has been brilliant and we have many CIOs from across the globe involved in the group. We have been pleasantly surprised with how active, open and collaborative the forum has been around these projects and we hope you enjoy the book.

In reading the submissions we noticed some merging themes: *transitions, transformation, global, career path* and *emerging trends and challenges* moving forward.

While there might be other important themes in future books, this book is organised around these themes:

- **Transitions:** Christian McMahon
- **Transformation**: David Knowles, Steve Homan, Chris Lord, James Mottram, Tony Walters, Peter Blower
- **Global CIO**: Kevin Robins
- **CIO Career Path:** Ken Towning, Paul Hobbs, Malcolm Lambell, Chris Michael
- **CIO Challenges:** Yiannis Levantis, Heena Prajapat, Pat Lynes, Abby Ewen.

We will be doing a series of these books, so if you're interested in authoring a chapter and would like to join *CIO 2.0* then please contact Pat Lynes on:

pat.lynes@sullivanstanley.com

We hope you enjoy the book as much as we have enjoyed putting it together.

Pat Lynes and Christian McMahon

CIO Transitions

The changing face of Technology Leadership

Christian McMahon

CIO 1.0 – IT Director Meets the modern world

The first evolution of the CIO role was to move it on from the "old school" IT Director approach of only being operationally focused and speaking to peers in a language centred around technology focused acronyms which is rightly no longer acceptable in today's boardrooms. That approach is viewed as old fashioned and those individuals perceived as purveyors of legacy infrastructure and outdated thinking, which doesn't chime with the commercially focused strategy of the modern organisation.

It also meant enrolling the CIO role into the C-suite alongside its peers and elevating the IT Director to a more meaningful commercial role to be delivered alongside the business as usual operational piece.

The trouble was the day to day operational piece naturally took up more time than the rest of the c-suite appreciated. This was especially true in organisations where the investment in its technology didn't match its commercial ambition and thus the time spent on the commercial side of the role slid a little, prompting more derision the CIOs way.

The savvier CIOs promoted their IT Managers in to Heads of IT, freeing up their time to concentrate on the commercially focused piece but many couldn't stop getting involved in the daily operational grind as this was their comfort blanket and truth be told what they enjoyed doing.

The Transformational CIO – The Change Agent

The CIO role has developed further with different flavours appearing which constitute organisations different ambitions on their technology agenda and it's not for the faint hearted.

Being a Transformational CIO is a tough balance to achieve, expected to drive their organisations in to becoming a digital first business whilst instigating a seismic shift in enabling technology to become a defining and differentiating strategic tool that can drive unparalleled commercial success.

They need to stay aligned with the overall strategic business direction whilst winning buy-in from all stakeholders and consistently delivering value focused change. In addition, they need to cut across lines of business, deliver new capabilities and open new pathways to success for sales, marketing, finance and more. They need to utilise their cross-business expertise to quickly understand the technological needs of the organisation and actively seek out opportunities to transform through building strong relation-ships across all levels of the organisation.

Above all, they need to act as a visionary, constantly seeking out the best technologies for their organisation be they current or emerging and understand how best to implement them to add the most value.

The Transformational CIO is naturally much in demand as many organisations want/need an individual who can develop and drive forward a technology strategy developed in harness with peers that can deliver their strategic objectives, improve the ways in which its staff work, increase agility, meet the needs of its clients and also provide a viable innovation agenda that delivers new product/services to market to increase competitive advantage. More often than not, the organisations that CIOs find themselves working in or joining do not have the above structure in place nor the capability to do so.

A large majority of the work I do is in developing and delivering large scale business transformation and change management programmes. These are not only the most complex programmes of work an organisation can undertake but also the most rewarding in a multitude of ways when they are delivered successfully.

Every high achieving CIO needs to have extensive transformation and change management experience as many of the roles they undertake will normally incorporate work of this nature.

The Interim CIO – The Gig Economy

This is the route I currently traverse and I am brought in to organisations in many guises including having experience in a requisite issue, needing to refresh/deliver a new IT strategy and/or target operating model and delivering significant transformation and change programmes.

Often, I am brought in by boards to bolster and/or augment the existing CIO through the delivery of a specific programme, enabling them to get on with other tasks. Other times I am brought in to a firefighting situation where things have gone wrong and the incumbent CIO has exited the organisation.

The skill of a good Interim is being able to have the requisite experience and capability to successfully deliver against any of these scenarios and at a far greater pace.

Contrary to popular belief, the Interim role is not the same as the old contractor model where you deliver a project and move on. The Interim seeks to build a relationship with their clients, enabling them to understand their commercial pressures and often going on to successfully deliver a number of programmes for them. An Interim can become a trusted member of the organisations armoury, being able to deliver significant return at a rapid pace when needed without being carried as a constant overhead.

Organisations often don't have the leadership capability they need to facilitate change and recruiting skilled Interims can allow organisations to successfully fill their capability gap and lead/deliver the requisite change.

Pat Lynes talks in more detail about the multiple benefits for organisations in using Interims in his chapter on the *Gig Economy*.

CIO 2.0 – The evolution of the CIO role

CIO 2.0 is my moniker for the newly evolved and commercially proficient CIO role that many organisations now require. It's the CIO who can speak the same commercial language as their peers, listen to and understand their commercial issues and strategic objectives whilst delivering relevant technology solutions to resolve them.

Equally important, is that this is also the incarnation of the CIO who wants to and is able to talk to your external clients. No longer can the CIO deliver technology products and services they 'think' will appease their customers, they need to talk to them, understand what they want and deliver it accordingly.

The major challenges facing today's CIO: The advent of digital

CEO's often ask me how can they become more digitally enabled or how can they better utilise technology to stop their organisation from being disrupted by smaller and more agile market players.

The obvious answer is that they need some form of business and digital transformation strategy that subsequently makes relevant changes across their organisation. However, there is so much more to consider such as are they delivering what their customers really want and in the right way? How can they utilise digital and other technologies to improve their products? Do they have a strong enough corporate culture to not only absorb but lead these changes through?

The appointment of a Chief Digital Officer is one way for larger companies to start to better formulate and put a working strategy around this whole area.

Personally, I see the Chief Digital Officer role as a transformation and change agent who will lead the digital transformation and implementation of a digital leadership culture within the organisation before bowing out gracefully with a job well done (puts on tin hat and hides under the desk from the digital brigade).

The CIO and others within the c-suite know their organisations and if they do their job properly, they also know their customers and what they want. The CIO/CMO axis is more than capable of delivering the digital agenda in the majority of organisations but if the company is majorly digitally focused or looking at a long term digital transformation then the CDO will need to join their ranks.

The cold reality is that 52% of the *Fortune 500* firms since 2000 are now gone.

This is not only attributable to a narrow focus on digital but it is most definitely attributable to companies who became complacent and ignored the market shifting around them which led to them being replaced by more disruptive market players.

Technology ownership and its orchestration across the organisation

Technology ownership and its operational control is now dispersed across organisations and the CIO needs to understand this should be embraced rather than wish them luck and hope they fail.

If the CIO doesn't grasp this proliferation of technology and respond to it, the business will often purchase and implement the technologies themselves, creating a shadow IT epidemic (sadly this is all too prevalent and highlights the fact the CIO is not listening to the organisation and understanding their critical technology needs).

This change in mind-set and approach is difficult for many CIOs to make, but the switch should free up their time, allowing them to focus on becoming a lead innovator and implementing positive change that eliminates inefficiencies and makes new, better things possible.

The changing state of enterprise technology

One of the key aspects of the CIO becoming a change agent within a business as a frontline deliverer of innovation both internally and for customers is to look at new and emerging technology which can free your organisation from the quicksand of its legacy systems and infrastructure, whilst improving process, strategic agility, mobility, availability of new features and above all, enable your staff to work more effectively.

No new technology platform has enabled this as much or created more column inches in recent times than the current proliferation of cloud services.

Almost every one of us is using the cloud multiple times a day to speak to our peers, store our data and access online services be it at home or at work. Despite its mainstream adoption, many of the CIOs I talk to are still relatively hesitant to fully embrace it, expressing concerns over security and control.

Unfortunately, it's this hesitance which can see CIOs often viewed as barriers to change, not listening to the critical technology needs of the organisation and fostering a *culture of no* based on inflexible, but long-established legacy systems.

In truth, it makes the CIO look out of date, not in touch with or interested in listening to the organisation and sadly it invariably leads to their exit.

Empowering your organisation and helping it retain/attract key talent

Forward-thinking CIOs who deliver technology services that enable organisations to offer flexible ways of working have a clear competitive advantage over those that do not. By offering the most up to date, innovative and flexible technologies, employees are more motivated in their day-to-day role as it shows that their organisation is investing in ways in which they can work more effectively.

Top talent also seeks the best working environments and I'm seeing more and more businesses position their IT flexibility, innovation and commercial agility as a major draw to would-be employees. These organisations are then left with a pool of top-talent across the whole organisation, driving extraordinary work and increasing business value.

Team Leadership and the Talent Agenda

Many of us would say we are good leaders and why not, we've done a lot in our careers and successfully led teams and delivered multiple projects whilst working our way up the corporate ladder.

But building great teams is so much more than that.

Creating trust is paramount and you need to be the leader your team deserve, giving them autonomy and seeking their guidance. You must also utilise the strengths of your team(s) as too many 'leaders' hire staff in their own image but guess what, that means you will always deliver the same things...

Teams are all about diversity of opinion and you need to foster an environment where that thrives through your influence and direction but remember if you let disengagement creep in, it will quickly spread and strip away all the good things you've done.

Conclusion

I've only just scratched the surface on many of these areas which rightly deserve far more airtime than I'm giving them here. In this piece, I wanted to highlight the main areas for what I think constitutes the changing face of technology leadership and the steps that CIOs need to take to add the most value to their organisations at this time.

I wish you the best of luck on your journey.

About Christian McMahon

Christian is a Commercially Astute CIO/CTO, Board Advisor, Global Business Leader, NED, Change Agent and Start-Up Mentor ranked as the 11th most influential CIO in the world.

Christian has a strong track record of success in permanent and Interim capacity at board level in challenging and rapid growth environments with substantial experience in VC (pre-IPO) and PE backed companies.

Christian is highly skilled in leading companies through transformation, turnaround, tech-enabled innovation, full M&A lifecycle, product overhaul, exit preparation and IPO (AIM/LSE/ NASDAQ).

He is an exceptional communicator and strategic thinker who can translate vision in to action and deliver better products, processes, services and technologies that enable more effective ways of working.

Christian has significant reach and influence across social channels and has worked with the world's leading brands, delivering significant commercial ROI.

As well as his work at the *European Commission* in being part of a technology panel for a €5 Billion technology and innovation fund, Christian is a global mentor at *MassChallenge, PWC's IncuBus Ventures* and China focused *Cocoon Networks* to start-ups across multiple industries and countries.

Christian has an amazing network and technology vista which allows him to constantly seek out the best technologies for organisations be they current or emerging and understand how best to implement them to add the most value.

Christian has extensive global board level private, public and non-profit sector experience including:

Expert in developing and delivering customer focused IT strategies that:

- Interpret corporate vision/strategy and translate objectives into tangible roadmaps
- Deliver Enterprise Cloud Transformation - On-Premise to Cloud Infrastructure
- Decommission legacy apps/infrastructure, modernise and re-platform to AWS, Azure, Google Cloud
- Lower the risk of sizeable corporate investments and improve ROI

Notable background in delivering digital business transformations and change initiatives that:

- Elevate performance, reduce cost, improve operational efficiency and facilitate new business models
- Build innovative, revenue generating digital products that deliver compelling customer experiences
- Design and implement target operating models delivering £mm impact

www.three25.com

christian@three25.com

www.linkedin.com/in/christianmcmahon

@ChristianMcM

CIO Transformations

The Quest for THE Silver Bullet

David Knowles

The search for the silver bullet that will give a company a disruptive, game changing point of differentiation is incessant. Yet even when an option is identified, successful implementation is rare. In reality, even business as usual programmes can surface issues inhibiting a company's ability to successfully embrace change. Why is this? Change is not a new concept, change is inevitable. Companies must embrace change to remain relevant and successful. It should be expected and good execution the norm.

Too often the fundamentals are not in place to set the organisation up for success. The following must be well considered and understood; motivation, ownership and accountability, opportunity choice, success criteria and the decision-making process.

- The motivation for change must be clearly articulated. What is the desired end state? Is the ambition to secure and improve the current product, serve an adjacent product or market, or be truly disruptive with a company, market and/or product context? This influences the type and source of disruption sought. It also informs the objectives, impact and success criteria before starting and allows these to be communicated.

It also starts to frame the execution early in the process. Change does not happen without effort, operational impact must be accepted and supported by senior management. Impact to the company's existing operations, ways of working and usual commitments must be allowed for.

To be successful the decision to embark on a disruptive journey must be conscious, informed and considered.

• With clearly defined motivation, the ownership and accountability may be obvious. But must also be accepted! An event driven by the CEO, therefore considered essential to the future of the company will typically enjoy different support than a CIO initiated technology change – which in reality few people will truly understand. Inevitably, when execution does not go to plan how the sponsor, senior management and company react in this situation is important and influenced by the accountability felt across the company and senior structure.

• The opportunity selected is important. Might sound obvious, however the choice is huge! Until recently, disruptive opportunities - particularly technology centric - would be proactively marketed by research companies. Following deep and detailed research, plotting the evolution and maturity of such opportunities to inform organisations why, what and when to adopt. These companies still have their place and are continuously refining their processes to remain relevant; however, they now complete with endless unicorn status chasing start-ups, immeasurable amounts of online information, or often simple impromptu casual conversations. Everyone has a view of the next big thing. Given the vast choice, it is easy to understand how an organisation can fail to decide, or back the wrong opportunity. Motivation is obviously a factor in choice, but ensuring a company has the right information on which to base a decision is also important. Choosing with the 'business as usual' visor on is unlikely to deliver disruptive change, insight both internally based on company vision, but also outside-in is important. Widening the market insight can really help disruption, for example if considering a change to customer interaction what looks good to a customer from outside your market? Customers define what good looks like from their last experience and don't care that the experience was not in your market. Learn from those that define what good looks like 'full-stop'- and be better.

•   Defining and agreeing the successful outcome of a project before beginning is project management 101, however often overlooked. This is equally true of retrospectively measuring the success, or not, of a project post implementation. With a transformation or disruption this is even more important as the usual success criteria may not apply. This is especially true if the source of disruption is truly company or market altering. But defining the business outcome is essential, it is OK if the success criteria cannot be articulated in detail at the outset. This may feel quite uncomfortable if the company is very figure dependant, so communication of the end goal, incremental delivery, incremental refinement of success criteria helps inform the questions that should be asked repeatedly. Is this the right thing to do?
Should we stop or change direction? These questions should be openly considered without fear of failure, even if a potential outcome is stopping the initiative.

•   Considering the research and allowing and enabling a decision is not as simple as it may sound. Chances are the organisation does not normally do this so to assume it can suddenly do this successfully is short sighted. This is a full-time role and therefore people need to be committed to it and removed from their day jobs. It is important to consider the execution in relation to current capabilities e.g. technology, people, process. This must be realistic, bottom up, not top down. It should not be assumed the current teams can make this happen. Even, perhaps especially, the CIO. Change is often difficult for the Technology teams to grasp, even though typically it is from these teams that change originates. Interim staff can help accelerate the learning, it is not that the people are necessarily wrong for the organisation, but an intervention is often needed to provide experience. Why learn on the job, use skilled, experienced resources who already have the battle scars?

Failure to consider these five factors inevitability results in unsuccessful delivery of disruptive technology, or at least to its full potential as recent history shows.

Consider *Big Data*, how many companies have delivered commercial success through this? *Service Oriented Architecture*, its premise to transform business by simplifying integration of legacy and modern platforms, has this really enabled quicker change? Mobile, what is your mobile experience with a company? Is commercial success being delivered through mobile or apps? Cloud computing ... Digital ... all these, and more, have promised game changing capabilities, and nearly all haven't consistently delivered.

Is it the concepts and promises that are flawed or the implementation?

The adoption of something disruptive will disrupt the organisation. We have already highlighted foundational changes necessary to prepare the organisation for the change. Assuming these are in place, let's consider execution.

To expect the as-is delivery capability to successfully deliver a major disruption or transformation is unrealistic. They are, typically, unproven in anything other than business as usual delivery. However, this is often lost in the excitement! The focus moves straight to the end state, with little consideration of how to get there. The organisation must equip itself to successfully adopt, integrate or otherwise make use of the incoming capability.

Without focus on this area the usual approach to delivery will be used. There will typically be a large up-front planning stage which will start to peel back the sales promises revealing reality. The technology integration is more complex, the business changes more challenging, or it is just bigger and more expensive than expected. Of course, at this stage there are still few facts, at best better-informed guesses.

This may prompt the conversation that the delivery model needs to be reconsidered, that a long drawn out delivery may not be the right approach, it may even prompt the question that the business as a whole needs to become more agile (small 'a') in its approach.

This is a positive realisation - especially if organisation wide - that things need to change, and that large disruptive transformation is not possible without fundamental organisational changes.

However, without clear leadership, the changes can typically be limited to the delivery teams and is implemented in one of two ways, neither of which will lead to a successful outcome:

- The internal technology team dust off an Agile (capital 'A') textbook and begin shifting into model Agile teams. Perhaps engage wider technology functions, introducing concepts such as DevOps. This will of course be successful, at least in the eyes of the technology team, they will be using Agile.

- The second approach, which may replace the first, or follow it if the first approach fails, is to engage an external consultancy. Senior (read expensive) consultants will parachute in and seek to embed their own version of Agile into the organisation. This is generally met with resistance from the internal teams hindering the process. This is typically a time bound engagement with the need to demonstrate success artificially limiting the agenda and scope.

Adjacent business teams and processes will need to change. Teams working to a fortnightly delivery rhythm collaborating with teams working to monthly or annual cycles will be at best suboptimal. It will cause each to have different expectations of Agile processes. The expectation that the Technology team can deliver everything they used to, plus they can squeeze a whole bunch of last minute changes in, they're agile now, right?

In my experience, the technology teams adopting Agile processes, the proliferation of white boards and Post-its is not what senior management envisage an agile (small 'a') organisation to be. A technology team using Agile processes does not make an organisation agile, ready to successfully embrace disruptive change. An agile organisation is the target outcome of more fundamental changes, not simply the adoption of a process.

This realisation brings the culture of the organisation into focus. This is another positive step towards successfully facilitating disruption, that simply adopting a process will not bring success. But how should cultural change best be approached? How can you measure when it has changed? What does success look like?

Cultural change is typically owned by the People teams involving workshops, mission statements, social activities, perhaps even new brands. Short, sharp bursts of effort and energy.

There are measurements associated with Agile process adoption, they can be used as a proxy for cultural change for example velocity of delivery, quality levels or accuracy of estimation/predictability of delivery and the more subjective feeling when attending the usual Agile rituals, or when something goes wrong. How teams react to problems is a great way to inform the degree of team accountability.

Cultural change at this level is very superficial, akin to making a company agile by adoption of an Agile process.

The changes needed to be successful are more fundamental. To deliver an agile organisation, able to adopt new processes and disruptive change, the focus must be on embracing behavioural change across the entire organisation. This is not about a disruptive project, this is about a disruptive organisation.

There are five behaviours essential to underpin what can be a seismic shift in organisational capability

- Accountability, remove the concept of a blame culture, everyone in the business must become outcome focused, in it together for the betterment of the company. One team. If something doesn't go to plan the entire team – Technology and the other business areas work together to solve it. I have never met anyone who has deliberately set out to fail, so my assumption is everyone wants to be successful. This sounds simple and should be, but non-value adding, self-preservation behaviours are typically deeply rooted and spread quickly.

- Collaboration, open forums, clear communication, speaking (really speaking, not Instant Messaging),

collaboration tools (Instant Messaging!), jointly working on something. The adoption of multifunctional teams with common objectives. Focused on success.
All roles required to deliver success actively engaged. Not engaged as in reading and signing an epic sized specification, useful only to be dusted off when things don't go as expected. Adoption of common simple language.

- Transparency, communication is king! There is plenty that needs to be transparent, beginning with the definition of agile. Working as one team there is no reason not to share good news and bad. If honesty is not the prevalent behaviour how can accountability truly be encouraged?

- Iteration, progressing in bite size chunks really drives home the reality that things change. The desire for wider change likely instigated the need to change behaviours. If something takes too long something else will have changed, that will impact the success. Early sight of what is being delivered encourages ownership and accountability. When things are not quite as expected, the resolution is a quick conversation and small alteration not unpicking months of effort.

- Constant feedback and improvement, one thing is certain, things always change. Change must be embraced, new technology, new concepts, new processes, new team members all present positive opportunity. This is a challenge, sometimes the very people responsible for huge amounts of organisational change are themselves very resistant to change.

That these behaviours will help organisations be success-ful should be common sense, and in turn will help support successful adoption of all Agile frameworks.

The actual Agile framework adopted is less important than establishing the right behaviours.

But more importantly they represent and support a change in culture that will allow an organisation to move forward.

This is a big shift, not everyone will like it, and it will not be instant, embedding behavioural change takes time. It is an iterative process, people embrace change differently, feedback and coaching are essential to support teams and individuals on the journey. The behavioural change extends throughout the organisation, including, especially, senior management.

Simply displaying required behaviours on posters is not enough, the behaviours have to be lived and demonstrated in all areas of the organisation.

All companies are different. Different cultures, technology platforms, technical debt levels, business and IT processes, the list goes on. However, the desire to be successful and to differentiate is consistent across all businesses – although what this looks like differs. People are the true asset of any organisation. To be truly successful therefore the focus in bringing about change has to begin with people.

Focusing on developing positive behaviours positions the company to take full advantage of any disruptive opportunity or transformation, enabling adoption of new process or technology. Organisations may even find focusing on behaviours in this way supports innovation from within, the creation of their own silver bullet.

About David Knowles

David is a highly experienced Executive technology leader with demonstrable success in all aspects of transformation, technology, digital, delivery and change.

He leads from the front, offering an inclusive, collaborative leadership style, taking his teams, stakeholders and senior management teams on the transformation journeys he has delivered.

Passionate about technology and its role in helping ensure deliver business success, David realises that this can only be done with the right team and has demonstrated the ability to recruit the right people and build successful teams throughout his career.

For the last 17 years he has held senior leadership roles delivering digital change within publishing, retail, ecommerce and financial services, the last year within the Interim market. His early career involved hands on software development within FMCG, consultancy and a software house.

David's background and passion for technology coupled with 30 years of successful technology delivery enables informed strategy creation and execution supporting transformation and business success

David holds a degree in computer science and an MBA.

Away from work, David is a committed husband and father, and enjoys airsoft and basketball.

https://www.linkedin.com/in/davidknowles

So you want to be a transformational CIO?

Steve Homan

A CIO transforming technology as a single function in my view is just a CIO doing their job. A transformational CIO is someone who plays a key role in the transformation of the wider business as well as the technology function. The nature and scope of that wider change will of course differ company to company and situation to situation, but the transformational CIO will certainly play a material part in making the change happen.

Being a transformational CIO is not an easy job. It often involves taking challenging, and sometimes unpopular, view-points or decisions. You are only ever as good as the last thing that went wrong (regardless of how true or in your gift to prevent), you have to take lots of personal risk, you are faced with impossible choices and often trying to get common sense to emerge from a sea of passive resistance. And you may not even have been hired to be the catalyst for transformation - but you recognise that it needs to happen.

So why do it - well it's a great challenge and deeply satisfying when it all comes together.

I have been through business transformation several times and have seen a clear pattern of what makes the difference and builds trust and momentum – that is the focus of this chapter - and hopefully it may help avoid making some of the spectacular mistakes I have learned from along the way.

The things I think need to be tackled to enable you to transform a company from the technology chair are:

- At all times over communicate and tell the story at all levels and to relevant teams

- Create a culture where everyone wins - by building a team that wants to win together

- Make sure there is a clear strategy - if there isn't one already, then get one in place no matter how long it takes or how painful it is

- Get brilliant basics in place

- Make the cost position clear and be clear on tech debt - it's about choices not perfection

At all times over communicate and tell the story at all levels and to relevant teams

A very wise man once said to me, "If you go to bed each night thinking you have over communicated, you might just have done enough." This is a mantra I work to daily. Open, candid and relevant communication is to me the foundation upon which you can build trust, reduce fear and provide clarity to your teams and colleagues. Each company has a different viewpoint based on geography, staff numbers, etc. - but I have found that establishing a set of routines is a good way to ensure everyone is aligned and gets on the path to the holy grail of respectful, candid two-way many to many conversation.

Establishing a routine and sticking to it always means that staff know when they are going to get information or a chance to ask questions. The more consistent and familiar it feels, the more a wider and wider group are prepared to join in. What do I mean by communication? I mean regular all hands style forums with many to many communication (i.e. question asking and debate is encouraged), informal gatherings on hot topics, daily cross-functional (tech and non-tech) stand ups, briefings from CEO, CFO, board members, smaller forums for in-depth briefing and debate on key topics. Tough topics should be called out and discussed openly, what is not working and challenges/risks should be balanced with what has gone well and it should all be delivered with a sense of candid fun.

It is an essential part of a transformation story that you help staff build the picture of what needs to happen and why, enabling questions and feedback. Fear, passive resistance and admiring long standing problems are often the biggest barriers to transformation - communication along with culture and strategy are your main devices to change those behaviours.

Create a culture where everyone wins - by building a team that wants to win together

I have often been asked how do you know if you have a good, bad or are changing culture - can it be measured, benchmarked and tracked - because that's how most management like to judge where they are at. But it is often false and leads to a nice blanket of placation being put over the top of tough deeply engrained problems.

For me, the answer comes from an honest appraisal of where you really are - and it is not something to which you can apply science. There is a clip on *YouTube* called *"The smell of the place"* where Professor Sumantra Goshal talks about being able to discern what kind of place you have walked into. We have all done it - pubs, hotels, other businesses. You quickly make a judgement about what kind of place it is – so, do this to your own business.

The things to look for are: how do people interact (functionally or helpfully)?, why are they there (money or purpose)?, are people working for each other?, what does the environment say about the activity being undertaken (quiet, noisy, messy, focused)?, what ceremonies exist that tell you who you are and how you are doing? How does it vary around the business? Are there examples of good and bad - what can be learnt from them?

So you have given this some concerted thought (ideally written it down) which means you should now have a sense of where you are - the next thing to do is to make some changes to foster the kind of culture you want. Over the years I have been through this loop a number of times and here is my playbook:

- Establish a meritocracy and know your people (I use a 9-box grid and review twice a year with the whole senior team reviewing all staff together). Those in the highest performing boxes should be positively actioned and the lowest performing should be reasonably supported. If there is no change in a quarter, poor performance should be dealt through a managed exit. It is a tough model, but I have always found this a key foundation to ensuring your teams know where they stand and that it is fair. During a transformation period, you are nearly always raising the performance bar and changing roles so it is an important temperature check.

- Reward often and with thought - rewarding the person not the staff member. By this I mean when thinking about rewarding for a great job, exceptional effort, etc. do not default to money as a measure - it lacks thought and is in-personal. Find out what works for that individual and do what you can to deliver it - I have bought a wide range of things over the years - family hampers, subscriptions, tickets, etc. - delivered discreetly to home with a handwritten note is always appreciated, unlocks discretionary effort and builds trust. The cost vs. value equation is overwhelmingly positive.

- Be open and candid about problems, challenges, wins and losses - over communicate it to as wider audience as possible and make it a two-way conversation.

- Take the time and make it a primary effort of you and your team to hire people who have the best possible mind-set, who bring something other than just required skills. I meet all but the most junior staff before we agree to hire them - it is not a yes/no meeting but a chance to understand what else they bring and their mind-set. You can do this in an open, fun 15 minute meeting and it means having sight of your incoming staff and the chance to ask questions if you are not sure. (I don't meet the most junior roles as it tends to create more stress for them so I leave that to others during the process).

- Be visible, vocal, open and helpful. Walk the floors (get on planes, trains and in automobiles) to make it happen. If your people see you as approachable without agenda the natural conversations are easy to start and you quickly get to the true picture. If I find reasonable gripes and grumbles I always personally make sure they are taken care of.

- Always support mistakes with a path to an answer when it is openly communicated - it is learning. Always treat any kind of hiding or politicking of facts with a direct and candid response - repeat offenders should be exited - it's just bad.

For me these five things together start to bring about the change in culture especially when teamed with open and regular communication and a clear strategy. Getting it working in your own function often leads to others taking note and copying.

Make sure there is a clear strategy - if there isn't one already, then get one in place no matter how long it takes or how painful it is

So, to strategy - done well it gives a company a purpose and a reference point against which to make decisions. Done poorly or not at all it creates confusion, false comfort and frustrates staff. Few executives seem to have a solid grasp of how to explore, define, document, communicate and execute strategy - often resulting in a noble sounding mission statement with a few short-term tactics.

As a transformation CIO, it is absolutely essential that a clear and well communicated strategy is in place - and not just a tech strategy - all sides need to be clear - product, commercial and tech. A well founded and communicated strategy provides a clear view of how it all fits together, it shows all staff what you need to do and why, and just as importantly it enables all to be clear on what you are not doing and why. So how do you go about it?

It can be boiled down to a set of processes and tools that can work in almost any environment - I don't have space to cover them in detail here (perhaps that's a future blog post) but here are the basics.

Go through the process of creating a Strategy Map. This is a well-documented and utilised tool that is the core asset in many high performing businesses. Some important points about the process:

- Set a clear expectation of the process and outcome - and the value of the outcome. Do not start unless you have buy-in to the outcome. If you encounter passive resistance it will often be based on fear so take the time to go through the rounds of 1:1 conversations until the fears are surfaced and clear.

40

- It must include participation from a reasonable number of the senior team to ensure co-creation and buy-in.

- It's OK to start with a rough draft to be finessed as a team.

- It will need multiple iterations - it's the iteration process where the logic and value comes out so expect to iterate and do it confidently. Sometimes it can be hard for senior teams to want to iterate but it really does help get to the best possible strategy.

The structure of the output varies but two essential aspects are:

- Your sources of sustainable competitive advantage - and a path to make them dynamic i.e., the people, processes and technology that make them up constantly evolving to constantly provide competitive advantage.

- How your tactics relate to strategies and how that relates to your goals/mission.

Once you have the version you are happy with this is where the transformation really starts and you can over communicate it. Then do it some more. And finally communicate it again just to make sure your entire organisation is clear on the direction of travel. My tip from the trenches on this one is to ensure others are the ones doing the communication as much as possible - it has to be visibly owned and driven by the wider organisation.

The final piece of the strategy jigsaw is to ensure that the strategy comes to life by re-focusing organisational measures and indicators directly to relate to the outcomes of the strategy. A balanced scorecard of lead, lag, trading and path towards strategic outcomes will give a rich picture of how trading for today is balanced against changing for tomorrow.

Get brilliant basics in place

By brilliant basics I mean that the core of the tech provision to the organisation provides what the consumers of it feel is needed - within given constraints - and importantly if there are compromises in meeting the constraints then they are well understood and communicated. This means helpdesk, device builds, printing, networking, Wi-Fi, app support, etc, etc, all need to just work - and that to be seen as a generally accepted fact - this is a strong foundation for building organisational trust which is vital. It does not need a grand plan, announcements etc, just solid service based on quality engineering. If this is not in place it will always come back and haunt you. What this means will be different in every company, but you gauge whether it is in place by making some calls, walking the floor - I try and do this often to temperature check what is going on - I always learn something new.

Make the cost position clear and be clear on tech debt - it's about choices not perfection

Finally let's address the usual CFO, CIO, CEO wrestling match around cost. It's always there in some form and in my experience if you are directly relating cost of change to the strategy map, you have brilliant basics in place and a quality team it becomes a much easier conversation founded on hard facts. Of course, the entry criteria is that you have good cost control in place and are able to transparently communicate changes.

I hope this quick canter through these topics acts as a useful catalyst to the transformation you are working on, are about to embark on or plan to embark on (delete as appropriate). It's not an easy task and it will involve tough days, lots of personal risk but the rewards are deeply satisfying. You won't get it all right, all of the time - expect to learn a lot from taking personal risk and making mistakes – I know I have for sure.

About Steve Homan

Steve loves to build teams that maximise what a business can be through the use of technology. He has taken on and successfully delivered turnaround, growth, IPO prep and transformation roles and has worked in the financial services, media, fitness, market research, utilities and management consulting markets.

Steve loves to work with businesses and management teams that have a strong impetus and mind-set to change.

He brings a sense of energy and passion and leads from the front to tackle technology challenges founded in clear strategy and creates a positive and ambitious culture.

stevehoman2@gmail.com

http://linkedin.com/in/sthoman

How to avoid walking into Transformation Treacle

Chris B Lord

Transformation is HARD, there are many books and articles on the subject. People who have successfully delivered a Transformation from start to finish are in high demand, they have the smart-cuts to ensure success.

Success starts at the very beginning of any engagement with identifying sticking points and building a plan to address them before making a clear-headed decision to take on the challenge, re-frame it or walk away.

Even seasoned Transformation executives can be caught by the gap between the right words and the wrong actions.

I have worked in different types of organisation, delivering Transformation within multiple industries and have seen that the danger of poorly understood Transformation is everywhere.

Here you will discover the danger signs and learn tools to ensure the change you deliver will be successful, be it a true Transformation or a powerful but incremental improvement. Critically, the change will be seen to be successful by the sponsors.

There are three basic sticking points to overcome before successful Transformation:

- Proving the sponsor really wants Transformation and all that entails. I will describe how to uncover the unspoken uncertainties and blockers.

- Ensuring correct stakeholders are bought in. The second section ensures you have the right environment and community to succeed.

- Discovering the gap between words and actions. I will describe some simple, early tests to uncover and address this.

None of these sticking points are technical. Change is not about technology, it is about people and their hearts, habits and interactions – if those are right then the right technology follows.

Is this what the sponsor really, really wants?
(Apologies to Spice Girls, 1996)

First step, does the sponsor understand what they are asking for.

I have been in conversations that start with "I want to Transform how we deliver great services to our customers" and after a few questions become "I want to keep doing what we're doing now but better, faster and cheaper AND I want to be able to talk about Transformation to the market and deliver some cool new services".

I call the second definition "Transformation Lite" and it is where the colour supplement school of Executive education really bites. There are many ways of exposing this sticking point and they generally revolve around the boundaries of what is to be Transformed, minimising the cost of Transformation or retaining core elements of the existing organisational processes, tools or structure. If this is what you hear, you need to very clearly reflect what you have uncovered and how your experience shows that attempting this change as a Transformation will lead to significant unhappiness and frustration. Use this analysis as an opportunity to reframe the engagement or potentially to walk away. Transformation Lite is the worst situation to try to land!

Secondly, does the Transformation address the key pain points of the organisation? It is easy to identify a critical risk to the company and also to want to Transform but unless the two are in support of each other, you will be spending a tremendous amount of time, effort and passion moving deckchairs around. To uncover this, talk to as many people as possible - senior, junior, suppliers and customers to understand the pain they feel and map it to the Transformation that is being sought. Once you have done that, you can expose the gaps to reframe and adjust the Transformation.

Are there any key emotional sticking points to slow down and gum up your Transformation? I refer to those parts of the organisation the sponsor is particularly proud of which they are especially worried about. These areas will almost certainly be hard to change and require significant understanding and communication because they elicit an emotional response in the sponsor. Logic alone will not win arguments, you will need to be very clear on the impacts to these areas through the Transformation and continually look for strong imagery to show benefits. You must NEVER brush these areas under the rug; they can derail your successes elsewhere.

Finally, does the sponsor recognise that the culture will need to change to embed the Transformation and ensure it endures? Ask how the company will feel after the Transformation, how it will make decisions and how it will deal with uncertainty. If there are no good answers then describe your view. This sticking point can be summarised as "It shouldn't be much different from today but faster and leveraging (insert cool tech here)". This is tricky to address as it is very daunting to accept upending something that has worked well to date. Logic and argument are unlikely to work so use the power of storytelling about the new culture and operating model tapping modern tools and methods.

Each of these, individually, is not a blocker to Transformation, it is the combination that will guarantee inertia wins, leading to recriminations and another change that didn't quite deliver. Transformation is about achieving an outcome for the organisation that benefits everyone. Doing anything less is not worth the pain or the effort.

It's hard to find the right people
(Ian Dury and the Blockheads, 1989)

Once you have understood the goal and aligned it into a Transformation, do you have the right people with you on the journey – not your team but community of stakeholders and influencers around you who will support or derail your Transformation?

First, is the sponsor the right person for the job? If the Board hasn't put one of their members into the role then they may not be really behind a Transformation. Transformation must have huge political capital and support behind it, which is beyond a mid-level manager. The sponsor should understand and have total control over the core area targeted for Transformation, this is not a good time to learn on the job.

The sponsor must not retain all their current responsibilities otherwise they will not have the attention to devote to all the air-cover and strategy work that they will need to devote to the change.

If the sponsor comes from a Board position and has been freed up, is there a risk this a 'Special Project' to move them out of the way? Check to see they still have influence and are well spoken of by other Board members.

Many of the investigations undertaken from understanding the sticking points will uncover additional concerns and allow you to have an open conversation with the CEO or Board on their appetite for Transformation. You should now have uncovered enough to build powerful word pictures of the right and wrong, good and bad approaches and outcomes.

If the right sponsor with the right influence and remit is in place, who have they got agreement from on scope and approach? I have seen situations where the CEO wants to transform but hasn't managed to convince the rest of the Exec yet doesn't have the political capital to replace them. You must talk to all the Exec and key Board members.

Depending on the size of the organisation, you must also talk to senior managers crucial to success in the affected functions and those they work closely with. Find out if they have clear roles and accountabilities in the Transformation, ask them to describe the benefit of the Transformation TO THEM. Reframe the Transformation for each key person and team so they identify and describe the benefits in their own words. This brings them into the process and will reap major benefits later.

A distinction between word and deed
(Die Kammer, 2016)

Discovering the gap between words and actions is the final step to delivering a successful Transformation. Simply asking questions will not uncover this dangerous sticking point, I will describe some simple, early tests to uncover and address this risk.

Find evidence of how the company and sponsor show their courage – do they do the right thing and put the effort into making it work or do they make frequent concessions?

A culture of compromises or 'special cases' is certain evidence of a mismatch between what is said and what actually happens.

Lots of decisions that are only partly implemented are a clear sign that hard decisions are often avoided or fudged.

A lack of governance forums which should be in place and the teams recognise as lacking is evidence of a fundamental gap in follow-through and accountability caused by a leadership that doesn't back up their words. If there are formal governance forums check they are attended by the right level of leadership to ensure they have teeth and they document and distribute their decisions AND EXCEPTIONS publicly and to all the affected people. If you can review old minutes then identify the number and distribution of exceptions around the company – this can help you find if there is an 'immune' team who get to do their own thing

Look for strange double reporting lines or people with junior roles reporting far above expected levels. Look for teams in unexpected structures.

Clearly you need to ask what the causes for these exceptions and it may be there are excellent reasons for them or you have been brought in to help address these complexities anyway but you need to push for the explanations to see if there is an endemic pattern that will be a hard nut to crack.

To address a difficult sticking point like this, you need to make allowing exceptions more painful than doing the right thing by either forcing them to be publicly registered or by showing the resultant increase in the actual cost.

Sadly, there is a limit to what you can do with a gap between word and deed. The gap between word and deed is generally down to a lack of courage which can't be easily worked around. Finding a deeply rooted gap between word and deed should be a red flag to help you decide if this is an environment where a real Transformation is even possible.

What next?

You should be clear if you now have a clear runway to succeed, if you need to reframe the Transformation as a set of incremental improvements to be handled as a set of small changes which create lead to Transformation OR if you should explain the situation and some remedies that need to be implemented starting at the Board and walk away until the organisation is ready.

I want to be clear – incremental improvements are fantastic, certainly not to be dismissed as worthless compared to the power of Transformation. What is more, they can be perfect building blocks before really starting Transformation and will increase the chance of success greatly.

Incremental changes can be delivered within current structures at lower risk. Obviously, there is less potential for return but never ignore the possibility to improve what you have in favour of chasing after headline-grabbing Transformation. The two can even co-exist.

Measurement is crucial and there are many articles on how to measure success. For me, the key is to tie the measures into the sticking points you uncovered above – if one team benefits from exceptions, make sure you measure the exceptions. If there are specific areas the sponsor is proud of and loath to change, make sure you track the Transformation of those areas. Return to each of the concerns you uncovered and measure every single one of them – a Board that sees the care you have taken tracking and mitigating risk will give you much more support.

Your honesty and insight is a crucial part of the success of Transformation but hopefully, my painful experiences in finding the sticking points above as well as how to uncover and address them means that you have some tools to give you the greatest chance of avoiding the treacle and driving an amazing Transformation.

References

- Die Kammer. (2016). *Word And Deed.* Delicious Releases.
- Apologies to Spice Girls. (1996). *Wannabe.* Virgin.
- Ian Dury and the Blockheads. (1989). *The right people.* WEA.

About Chris B Lord

Chris B. Lord has worked in Technology for over 25 years delivering leaner, more responsive and more impactful technology across many industries.

He is using that experience at Collinson Group to drive new services that support mass-affluent travellers globally. Integrating the company's skills in Full-service Marketing, Loyalty Platforms, Insurance and Assistance and Lifestyle Benefits, he is expanding the impact of Collinson brands such as Columbus Direct and Priority Pass.

As part of his career, he worked in the USA for seven years and managed teams spread across Asia, Australia, Europe and North America, he speaks fluent French and passable American.

His main roles include *Reuters* where he ran the Fundamental and Reference Data services, Head of Technology at *DST* (a major global financial services supplier) where he was responsible for the re-design and re-architecture of two core products, culminating in five industry awards. He then took a role at *dunnhumby* where, as CTO, he was responsible for innovation in the Customer Analytics space using Big Data techniques to drive product strategy for Social Media Advocacy, Pricing and Promotions, and Customer Insight.

https://www.linkedin.com/in/chrisblord/

Selling the value of Digital Transformation: tactics for the boardroom

James Mottram

Transformations are about delivering value. Whether its developing a new product line to meet customer needs, increasing market share through acquisitions, achieving cost reduction through shared services, and so on; transformations are necessary to execute strategy and ultimately deliver value to shareholders.

Many business and technology leaders are well practiced in identifying transformation opportunities and conveying their potential value to the board. These transformations are often within or on the periphery of the existing business model i.e., the ecosystem of processes, customers, suppliers and systems, which deliver value today.

Relatively recently however compute power, storage and network bandwidth have reached an accessibility, scalability and price point whereby when combined effectively they can enable new business models that weren't possible or viable previously. Companies which seize this opportunity and are quick to leverage these capabilities can compete and even overtake established incumbents.

Digital transformation is unlocking value through new business models everywhere we look, for example; *Tesla* extending the range of their customers cars to support the hurricane Irma evacuation, insurance companies such as *John Hancock* and *Cigna* reducing premiums through wearable device enabled wellness programmes, *IBM* Watson increasing the speed and accessibility of legal search through Artificial Intelligence.

In these examples, we can see that in addition to the targeted application of digital technology to create value, they are also redefining the sector or even industry they operate in; a car manufacturer trading on customer service rather than units, insurance companies extending into preventative healthcare (with a knock-on impact to pharmaceutical sales?) and a technology company democratising expert legal capabilities. This is not to be confused with the digitisation of existing business processes and ways of working.

Digital transformation has far greater and wide-ranging ramifications.

Fast forward to the not so distant future of autonomous electric vehicles and this one innovation will redefine the Automotive industry, with consumer ownership replaced by fleets of vehicles offering journeys as ad hoc transactions. There will also be significant repercussions to energy, insurance, travel and infrastructure planning and management.

The availability of digital technology creates a new paradigm of business opportunities and whether its five years or 25 years, all businesses will be digital businesses in the future and the effects will be felt in every business now or very soon.

Transitioning from traditional models of value creation to digital models is not straightforward. Conveying the value and creating a sense of urgency to invest in changing how the business operates, injecting new skills and changing culture across the organisation, is a big task.

Responses for established industry incumbents include experimentation, incubators, partnering or acquiring start-ups but how to go about selling this to the board or converting from these more peripheral approaches to embrace digital transformation at the core? What tactics might be deployed to achieve success?

Identifying the digital dynamics of the industry

Digital transformation promotes change within and across industries. What are the changes happening today and in the future and how might value be created from digital transformation as it relates to your business?

In the case of Renewable Energy, a tipping point has been reached where it is now cost competitive or even cheaper than traditional forms of power production, disrupting established incumbents and markets. We can expect renewables to continue this trend with new business models enabled by digital technology. Not unlike automotive, manufacturers are moving to provide total life warranties of hardware, enabled through enhanced turbine condition monitoring capabilities underpinned by internet connected sensors, big data and advanced analytics. Where surges in energy demand once meant expensive flashpoints to increase supply, demand side response technologies can today reduce industry demand and balance the grid by turning down refrigeration or heating plants, for example, in real time.

Digital transformation has already fuelled the rise of the sharing economy and the prosumer. *AirBnB* has achieved a valuation as much as *Hilton* and *Hyatt* combined by forming a marketplace of our rooms, flats and houses.

In the near future, we will be able to use batteries in our homes (or even the batteries in our electric cars) to supplement photo voltaic solar roof tiles on our houses, reducing demand for power from the grid, and providing the potential to sell excess energy produced to our neighbours, all securely transacted via blockchain. Who will seize the opportunity to own this marketplace and be the "*Energy AirBnB*"?

Digital transformation enables businesses to create value upstream and downstream of their current position within the industry and at the intersection of industries, customers and suppliers (Venkatraman 2017). Therefore, value propositions from digital technology require us to think beyond our current business operating model, sector and even industry.

Modelling this to show the current trends and likely future shifts in the market can be a powerful tool to communicate how the customer and competitor landscape is changing as well as starting a dialogue on what it means to the business for both strategic risks and opportunities, as existing sectors become more competitive or new sectors for value creation emerge.

Understanding readiness for change

Are the conditions favourable for change to be accepted i.e., is the board likely to be receptive and are they ready for change? Is there a sense of importance and urgency for digital transformation?

Most successful industry incumbent businesses are well established and so are entrenched in process, policy, culture and KPIs, which to some extent proliferate and sustain the status quo. There may not be an obvious burning platform evident in the current results and future forecasts (if based on historical trends) are unlikely to provide one either.

For industry incumbents, the appetite for change of this scale may be limited.

The less ready for change the more groundwork may be needed, shifting how individuals on the board think about digital technology opportunities relative to their business. Consider the influencing factors, for example; most boards are incentivised to manage businesses to deliver repeatable stable returns for shareholders, at an acceptably low level of risk. Governance, controls and strategic planning processes are honed for this purpose. On the surface, digital transformation can appear in conflict with this.

However, using the same factors which influence the board today in a different context can give the case for digital transformation a significant shot in the arm: where is the cross over point where inaction on digital transformation becomes a greater risk than action? What are customers demanding today and in the future how will a more personalised, flexible and lower cost service be provided without digital transformation? What are the market forces which are likely to come in to effect in the future; competitor innovation replacing current profitable patents held by your business today or reducing subsidy or reduced demand due to industry intersection driven substitution (our insurance/wellness/pharma example above), which can be mitigated through embracing digital transformation? Additionally, who are your competitors in a digitally enabled world and what are their strategies?

These are important questions and if no one on the board can answer them then the door is open for collectively reconsidering the services provided by the business today and how technology is utilised. Confirm who in the organisation is leading on strategy development, competitor analysis, key account management and risk management and look for opportunities to collaborate with them to add a digital dimension to their output, raising awareness outside the technology function along the way.

Driving shared ownership at the board

Is sponsorship alone sufficient to mobilise the business to maximise the opportunities of digital transformation, or is a more fundamental shift in ownership needed?

There is a common dynamic where the technology leadership of a business (Chief Information Officer/Chief

Technology Officer/Chief Digital Officer) are tasked with *"managing technology for the business"* or *"ensuring we have a digital strategy"*. The technology leader's role at the board is often one which supports the existing business strategy and operating model, developing propositions on how technology can improve business performance.

Typically resulting in investments to enhance current capabilities: customer relationship management, reporting and analytics, mobile enablement, supply chain management etc. This type of dialogue with the board perpetuates the technology leader's position as technology advisor or support function leader, responding to the business strategy, and not a business leader working in collaboration to create new digital enabled business strategies.

This segregation of technology and business leadership can also have implications for the preparedness of the other board members. What is their level of familiarity with digital technology and the use cases for value generation? The days of wrestling pocket diaries from directors to replace them with smart phones are behind us but how many members of the board engage in social media, one of the earliest examples of digital technology, enabling customer engagement and personalisation?

Such is the pervading nature of digital transformation, shared ownership across the board is required. This is a more fundamental change than sponsorship, embedding digital in the fabric of the organisation. Instead targeted sponsorship can be used to drive specific initiatives or projects. In this scenario, a key part of the technology leader's role is to develop the framework for digital transformation and coach other senior business leaders on when to get behind a new opportunity and what organisational capabilities will be required to make it a success.

Relating to the audience

How best to relate the unfamiliar subject matter of value creation from digital transformation and make it relevant and impactful to the audience?

Most board members will be familiar with, and most businesses use, established frameworks and methodologies for strategy development or strategic planning.

When considering digital transformation's effects on an industry or industry intersection could Porter's *5 Forces* (Porter 1979) be used to analyse the industry, new entrants, substitute products and so on?

When forming the argument that the responsibility for digital transformation should be across the entire board, and necessitate a change in ways of working across the entire business, Drucker's *"Culture eats strategy for breakfast"* is likely to resonate. Could McKinsey's *Three Horizons of Growth* (Baghai, Coley, White 1999) be used to illustrate how competitors are responding to the urgency of digital transformation by developing all three horizons in parallel? And where are we on Kotter's *8 steps for leading change* (Kotter 1996) on our digital transformation journey?

Making the case and demonstrating the value of digital transformation can feel like an uphill battle. It is likely though that there are allies on the board, and the opportunity to bring the case for change to the business in partnership should be exploited. It's not just the IT leadership who will be feeling the pressure to illuminate digital transformation for the business; CEOs, COOs, CMOs, Strategy directors and others will all have digital on their agenda and feel the burden of digital transformation.

Collaborating will enrich the case for change through current customer, competitor and operational delivery relevance, add credibility and start to gain the early buy in needed for successful delivery.

The skills to link digital enablement to business strategy and provide practical delivery paths may not currently exist in the organisation.

A combination of channels provides a range of expertise to be deployed as needed on the digital journey: seek out digital practitioners in formal and informal networks for lessons learnt, partner with expert third party support for targeted strategy or delivery engagements, build internal capability through the digital courses from the likes of *Boston University* or *Harvard Business School* and work with digital start-ups to see first-hand how digital enables rapid scalability. Where possible raise the exposure of key stakeholders to these channels too, through shared engagements or joint coaching.

The opportunities for digital transformation are there for the taking but the clock is ticking. Digital business models enable agility.

Until 2012, *Tesla* had only delivered the *Roadster*, a low volume niche electric car, today their valuation has overtaken *Ford*, they have the world's largest battery factory, the *"Gigafactory"* in Nevada.

It's an exciting time and business leaders have an important role to play in embracing and shaping how our digital world evolves. Start-ups and digital first businesses have stolen a march on this territory but established industry incumbents have the resources to maximise the benefits of digital transformation.

Unlocking the potential relies on combining industry dynamics, creating urgency to act through shared change ownership and selling the case for digital transformation in a way which resonates with the board and enables change in the business.

Bibliography

- Baghai, M. Coley, S. White, D. (1999) *The Alchemy of Growth. Practical Insights for Building the Enduring Enterprise*. Perseus Books.

- Kotter, J. (1996) *Leading Change.* Harvard Business School Press.

- Porter, M. (1979) *How Competitive Forces Shape Strategy.* Harvard Business Review

- Venkatraman, V. (2017) *The Digital Matrix.* Life Tree Media Ltd

About James Mottram

James Mottram is a business leader with extensive experience in both the private and public sectors, having lead IT for the likes of *Balfour Beatty, London Underground* and *Renewable Energy Systems.* He is also the co-founder of digital communications consultancy, *Rolling Thunder,* and a board advisor to a number of start-ups and rapid growth organisations, including *GrowthEnabler.*

With a unique blend of technology, innovation, strategy and digital expertise, James has a track record of leading global business transformation, resulting in tangible positive impact on profitability, performance and market results.

Currently Group CIO of *Renewable Energy Systems*, the world's largest independent renewable energy company, James has built a reputation for driving business impact through successfully combining digital innovation, customer-centric solutions coupled with organisational change.

www.linkedin.com/in/james-e-mottram

Journey to Transformational and Digital Interim CIO

Tony Walters

The Chief Information Officer

The Chief Information Officer role is one of the most rewarding positions anybody could ever wish for in their career however, it can be a scary experience on your first appointment. The sudden increase in responsibility and decision making must be akin to diving in the deep end of the swimming pool having never learnt to swim and looking for the life buoy ring!

The level of communication and commitment is multiplied significantly as is your level of influence. Your stakeholder collaboration must reach new heights and you must stay objective, impartial and always doing the right thing at all times. We must also not forget the all-important customers whose expectations are even higher than anybody around you in delivering an exceptional service irrespective of the situation. You are a C Level business partner, the custodian of budget, owner and manager of risks and most time the innovator of the leadership team. I like to call it the *"hot seat".*

As a CIO, there are also those challenging times you are scratching your head like Stan Laurel to find answers to the unexplainable situations. Character building, I think is the expression!

On the flip side, the CIO position is so very rewarding. Completing a new integration or delivering a new service and we must also not forget the important innovation programs. All give an emotional buzz for all involved to share. It feels like what I always dreamed as a boy to what it must be like to lift the FA cup at Wembley with the crowd cheering around you and in addition, you scored the winning goal!

In my career, I have been honoured to have worked with some astonishingly smart, talented and influential people at all levels including public figures. I have learnt lots from all of them on my journey and one of the key learnings is that of commitment. To be able to commit you have to be devoted to the role, your team and the business you are working within. You spend fifty percent or maybe more of your time in the office, so it is essential to have passion.

It is not a job, it is a way of life even if that results in sleeping in the office occasionally when things are not going to plan. The unwanted result is the unfortunate intrusion into family life. I have lost count of how many family holidays have seen me on the phone dealing with an issue or flying back on a plane to direct real emergency situations and then returned to the calm of the beach once the emergency is resolved. My very patient wife always quotes to me that at least I made it for the birth of my children!

My Technology and Leadership Journey

My technology journey began in a college classroom attentively learning the theory of bits and bytes to become an engineer. During my early career, I had managers who had identified potential in me and pushed me painfully past what I believed was possible. I am experienced working in application development, infrastructure, cloud and also managed some large programs as a project manager. Each step resulting in more time in the class room and a certification of some kind. Thankfully, I was also trained to be a manager, and this has proven to be the most valuable period of learning in my career. To me, that has been more valuable than an MBA.

The majority of my technical journey was in the highly regulated financial industry but once I made the exciting but scary transition to CIO, I found myself moving away from the finance vertical into supply chain, distribution and retail by entering as a regional CIO and then onto group CIO and entering the boardroom. A new door had opened and I began the next journey of building lasting commercial relationships.

Experienced CIO

Winding the clock forward, I have been an International CIO for a while now working in many counties. I have experienced a wide range of subjects from IPO, business sales, many M&A situations and working in VC and PE backed organisations along the journey. All great learning experiences with different challenges at each and every step.

As trends seem to change and develop, the role or title of the CIO has now become blurred and could be called the *Chief "Innovation" Officer* or even *Chief "Digital" Officer* as focus on digital transformations moves up the list of critical paths as businesses look for an advantage and to automate as many processes as possible with a positive impact on the balance sheet. The reality is that both innovation and digital programs have been a part of the CIO role for many years and experience tells you the biggest challenge of digital transformation is positioning the board room for investment. Knowing all perspectives and understanding risks is key to approval and thankfully, over the years, I have built a very solid strategy around this area and also around the cultural disruption the journey will cause to the organisation.

Like many others, during the CIO journey, I have developed my own brand. A situation that was not planned in any way. I have considered entering the Global CIO awards many times, but my CEO's would always tell me the same thing to put it on the back burner until a specific task has been completed. In speaking to one of my CEO's one day, he told me it was his nice way of saying he does not want all of the company's strategy and achievements posted for all to see. To this day, I respect the situation and refrain from these situations as much as possible even though I am told of my strong ability to influence change.

Change of Attitude in the Board Room

During my CIO journey, I have seen many changes and trends come and go but one such change caught me by surprise. A board room generally has a set tempo of outcome with a set process of getting things approved and you learn how to approach with the best outcome. I usually find the non-executives offer a great balance to risk and reward and can be a great asset and partner technology. However, around 2010, I begun to see an immense change of direction. Traditionally, large consultancy firms were always considered safe hands for larger projects, but I could see a trend of using an experienced Interim becoming the preferred route. A proven expert if you like with more flexible approach.

By 2013 I had seen this change of judgement numerous times which influenced me to make the transition for myself and moved out of the corporate comfort zone and made the leap into Interim Transformation CIO to find as many FA cup lifting opportunities as possible.

A new journey was about to begin!

The Interim CIO

I have always considered myself a transformational CIO even before the title seemed to appear a few years back. This is a key area that as a CIO, you are tasked to steer the business forward using technology and you need to know what technology is foundation layer and an enabler so that you make sure your roadmaps and budget is always focused on the reward.

There are three areas I specialise on and that is digital, cloud, and process realignment. Having worked for some vast and progressive organisations, I have also driven a significant number of M&A programs. Surprisingly, these also lead to transformation opportunities. All these areas have multiple options depending on the business vertical and regulatory challenges ahead and it has to be noted that not one size fits all, but the outcome on each of these transformations areas can be astonishing and rewarding.

One of the biggest and most positive changes I have witnessed is that Interim opportunities are far more focused on the ability and experience of the candidate rather than the industry segment they come from. I always frown now when I see job descriptions saying, *"must have sector experience"*. I call this "sector blindness" as it can have a negative and costly impact to any sector who have no view to a solution of a problem that is already available elsewhere. Thankfully the trend for the experienced and exceptional recruiters now is to remove the exposure of sector blindness and promote the cross pollination of knowledge.

It is just under four years ago I made the leap across the chasm to an Interim Transformation CIO, and currently have three successful *"gigs"* under my belt.

Each gig has been within a different industry solidly supporting my theory on having very transferable knowledge across multiple business verticals. Each one has been digital transformation focused both on front and back office with cloud migrations included in each position. Each have been large scale transformations with one position driving change across 16 separate countries adding culture and HR regulatory challenges into the mix.

Permanent V Interim – The Major Differences

Having made the leap, I have witnessed two key differences between the permanent role and the Interim. Firstly, that of accelerated change requirements. As an Interim, as an example, if you are taking temporary responsibility for the technology department, you don't have the luxury of the 90-day evaluation and plan. You have to be significantly more organised, use your experience to a heightened degree and be more clinical in the way you work with your team. You are there to deliver something very specific in most cases and you need to cut through the trees, walk past any politics and focus on the task much quicker that you have been used to.

The second difference is that of variety. Of the three gigs which consist of healthcare, sales, distribution, manufacturing and logistics, the healthcare gig was the most varied and rewarding experience so far.

A vast and complete digital transformation of front and back office including legacy process and implementation of mobility products with a challenging integration back to the NHS. Selling the solution to the board in this case was painless and the faces in the room when I presented an application developed taking less than 5 minutes to complete scheduling will remain with me for a long time! This would normally take around 10-12-man days per location!

These are the rewards that count especially in a healthcare environment where costs and efficiency drive the service and give a significant advantage over any competition. It can also save lives! In this case the many could see the impact on jobs post automation up and down the country.

Managing that situation was as rewarding as the innovation of technology. As far as healthcare goes, I would do this project again and again as the feeling of giving back is just outstanding.

For me this was the gig providing me the FA cup experience I always dreamed of!

Would You Make the Move to Interim?

It is easy to conclude that being an Interim requires many factors to be taken into account. Where you are in your CIO career and what you can bring to the table has to be core to the decision. I believe that as an Interim, you are a consultant in nature and not just in name which we are all used to seeing in our industry.

When considering the leap, you have to remember as an experienced CIO you are sitting on such a knowledge base that needs to be exercised at every opportunity to keep it current. We all know how fast our industry evolves and as an Interim, you have to be at the front of the evolution curve at all times.

Exercising your knowledge is both rewarding and fun and after all, we all need something to make us jump out of bed every day and go home with a smile. For me, serving as an Interim Digital Transformation CIO hits the spot!

About Tony Walters

Tony has been a senior technology professional for over 25 years. Tony started his technology career at the *London Stock Exchange* and continued working in finance industry for brands such as *Barclays* and *Morgan Stanley* eventually progressing to become the CTO of *ICAP* in London.

Tony went on to become a founding partner of the telecoms software platform now trading as *Flexenet* which has revolutionised the speed of delivery of trading services and disaster recovery on a global basis.

Tony has continued to hold various CIO positions around the world for some of the world largest International organisations including Ingram Micro and Brightstar based in the USA and central Europe where his focus has been on optimising business process with digital technology for the business to stay ahead of the competition.

Tony has recently completed assignments as an Interim CIO in both the UK and the USA which he has used to harmonise his knowledge transfer between business sectors. This has allowed Tony to carry out a large and very successful digital transformation in healthcare and also a large technology refresh program introducing technologies like augmented reality to a legacy retail experience.

Tony is based in the UK and is married with two children and spends his spare time in his passion for cars. He is also a keen F1 and Football fan where Tony can usually be found watching Millwall on a Saturday.

Tony was born and educated in the UK.

tony.walters@bright-technology.co.uk

https://www.linkedin.com/in/tony-walters-6844384/

Getting off the "Transformation Merry-Go-Round"

Peter Blower

Stating the obvious

Over the last decade, many longstanding, successful companies have found themselves fighting for market share and fending off disruptors in their industries. New entrants or sometimes existing competitors have been connecting more effectively with customers, driving change in the sector at a much faster pace than ever before. This is old news, but it has still not been enough to shock some organisations into fundamental change. It's not that they haven't tried. CIOs are often hired to drive such transformational change, but while some transformations do succeed, many do not.

Much has been written about the failings of business transformation programmes, generating vast amounts of content for both consultants and conference agendas alike.

Any *Google* search creates more entries than anyone would care to read, so it's easy to understand exactly what we should be doing to deliver successful change and transformation. There are plenty of easy to follow, good practice guidelines that readers can translate to their own organisation, and as a result, many organisations have improved their mechanisms to deliver change programmes, but perhaps not transformation.

We all know what we need to do…right?

We know the obvious things that need to be in place - vision, coalition, unity in the cause, a sense of urgency, great communication, dedicated managers driving the change and so on. Despite all of this, I still see too few examples of positive long-term change in organisations. Changing 'the way we do things around here', gets overlooked. Did the knowledge and skills required to drive these new behaviours become embedded? Was the real issue really tackled? Was the real issue even identified?

The Transformation Merry Go Round
Step 1 - The Grand Idea

Whilst we can all identify the leading tech companies and industry disruptors in the world, in reality, many of us work for organisations that don't fall into that category. Our companies may talk internally about being leaders, big brands or powerhouses from the last few decades, but in reality, many are somewhere between marginal growth and decline. In those industries where disruption is starting to bite, transformation is inevitably a hot topic.

Those responsible for strategy can well articulate the perceived gaps in their product or proposition in light of new entrants and disruptors. They know what customers think of products in the market, and the problems that need to be addressed.

Inevitably, this creates the need for new strategy due to the *"burning platform"*, the catalyst for change. The transformation programme is born. *'We need to up our digital game.' 'We need to catch up and change the company.' 'This transformation is the catalyst for us to behave differently.'* We've all heard, read and maybe even uttered such statements. The grand idea and the transformation programme is launched.

Transformation Merry Go Round
Step 2 - Downsize the Grand Idea

Many transformation projects start out with grand ideas, but over the course of time, end up being more narrowly focused on timelines and deliverables for a specific event or product. After all, most leadership teams generally know what needs to happen on the surface to make the go-live or launch occur. Whilst it can sometimes be fraught and stressful, this is the easy bit to control and manage.

The lasting cultural change that should have been identified at the inception of the transformation is for the most part difficult to scope, implement, and hard to measure as a return on investment. Too often, the focus ends up being on a one-time change to a channel, a proposition or a product.

It's hardly surprising. Being placed in a leadership role for a major transformation programme often means the CEO has great belief in that hire, after all, he or she could be the one to rescue the company. This can however, make or break a career both internally and externally too. The stakes are high and soon, as everyone starts to feel the pressure, the seeds of failure are sown. Timelines become tight and at times, unrealistically short, as results need to be delivered quickly. The 'long term' gets left behind. The short-term deliverables and date for 'launch' are in the spotlight.

Inevitably, in this pressured scenario, some will suffer damage during the delivery phase, others will claim victories and the identified product or proposition 'gap' will have been narrowed or closed (for now).

Failing to fix 'what's wrong with us'

The problem with all this anguish and effort is that the end result is limited, and not the lasting, change we'd all hoped for. Transformational change never really got the focus it needed.

All that's happened is that we ran off to IT and asked them to build something new. After all, it feels less risky to boil it all down to a tech change for a product gap, as opposed to tackling the culture and all those other intangible, immeasurable aspects.

I continually see insufficient discussion and analysis around why the gap between propositions got so wide in the first place, and why the company can no longer compete. Many of those conversations are just too uncomfortable for the incumbent leadership. Without addressing this, we end up in a series of one off *'transformation'* programmes, which never deliver on the true issue. This is the "Transformation Merry-Go-Round".

Inertia and knowing the new direction

Some businesses have continued in a similar vein for decades, enjoying high margins and paying handsome dividends. Now though, often due to complacency and a lack of knowledge about current trends, are finding themselves several years behind. They are competing and wrestling against competent digital businesses. They recognise that change is the new norm and they need to adjust somehow to compete, but without truly understanding the radical changes occurring around them, they can't effectively respond. After all, if you haven't been exposed to how the new market leaders operate first hand, it's hard to know what you're striving for.

There are many established leaders who have little idea of the kind of cultures their newer, younger competitors are enjoying in leading digital businesses. The tendency is to run off to the consultants, so they can show us the path, (because we can't find it), or taking extra notes at that conference, with the slide outlining "what makes the Amazon culture successful". This isn't going to solve the problem.

What this change looks like is hard to visualise. How can we quantify mind-sets and attitudes, employee's understanding and level of interest and engagement in the digital economy, or culture in digital businesses? Outside, looking in, it can be easy to see there is a problem, but for those internally, it's much more difficult to know where to start.

Sumantra Ghoshal outlined some of the problems in a talk that's available on *YouTube* called *'The Smell of the Place'* and is worth a watch.

I have heard organisations proudly talk about their levels of retention, their dedicated workforce and their strong culture. I think this element of pride in 'what we have built' is especially true in historically successful organisations, but is that culture adapting or remaining static? Are organisational structures, decision making speed and collaboration adapting to the new norms?

Setting your new direction

It can be difficult to know which is the right path for your own organisation. There are numerous digital maturity assessments and frameworks out there that may even measure hundreds of points in your business to identify your current state, and there are many skilled individuals to help you move forward. Whatever the method you choose for transformation, upgrading technologies and products is not enough.

We need an honest conversation about where we are now, why we are in this position and how willing we are to take the initial pain that will really lead to change.

HR can play a major part in leading an organisation through this process, with broader training and organisational design that moves away from some of the traditional structures and decision-making processes.

The disruptors in the market are hiring the top talent, and some new talent is clearly desirable - people with different mind-sets, attitudes and working knowledge of today's market.

Where this isn't always possible, developing and retaining existing talent is an equally critical component, as competing for the very best talent will be challenge.

Can your leadership team navigate?

The leaders in our organisations need to re-learn the way we do business today. They may have great experience and leadership skills, but they need to understand tomorrow's marketplace. They need to be able to recognise that some of the old methods from yesterday are no longer serving the interests of the company and shareholders. How do you achieve the pace and agility of a start up? How do you service the endless stream of customer needs?

Others in the organisation maybe the best navigators

If we're looking for inspiration internally, maybe some of the drivers of change are already apparent. I've seen many examples of those with newer mindsets, digital natives, generation y (whatever terms you choose) wrestling for more autonomy and empowerment or fighting against overly rigid frameworks. This friction is not hard to find in many companies. Coupling their mindsets and understanding of the marketplace, with the leadership and coaching ability of established leaders can be a powerful combination, but needs a senior team willing to be coached too.

Renewal

There are of course great examples of companies that are achieving the deep, cultural change that's necessary. In most cases it took a visionary CEO and a like-minded HR leader, setting a direction and successfully changing culture through a variety of methods over time.

It maybe all or some combination of reorganisation around product teams, new open plan offices encouraging communication and collaboration, changing business processes, hiring staff from a variety of companies in the more disruptive parts of the economy - those that have already experienced and led this change, that have built teams in other organisations and upgraded both talent and digital capability.

Changing recruitment policies and performance management processes, managing diverse groups of people, are also factors. There are many areas that need to be tackled.

The good news is that there has never been an easier time than now to bring in brilliant talent from the contract market and Gig Economy, to infuse and develop existing teams and to help break down those barriers that have always slowed or even prevented progress and innovation. Dressing down, bean bags and multi-coloured walls aren't sufficient. We need to create an environment where talented people want to be and to stay, where they can continue to develop, learn and genuinely influence the organisation's direction.

The key here then is not only being able to identify the problem, but having the boldness and vision to tackle it. Disruptors and leading competitors will continue to improve too, so if business feels tough this year, imagine how it will feel next year.

One of my favourite quotes comes from Jack Welch. 'If the rate of change on the outside exceeds the rate of change on the inside, the end is near'. It's time we moved away from channel led transformation to true transformation. The goal is the cultural shift, equipping us to effectively compete and take on the disruptors. It is only in this environment, or on the journey towards it, that the transformational CIO can have real and lasting impact and we can at last get off the *"Transformation Merry-Go-Round."*

About Peter Blower

Peter Blower is an IT leader with a track record of enabling companies to quickly scale and grow their businesses by fixing and transforming their IT functions. Pete is passionate about building and coaching IT teams, consumer facing technologies and business strategy.

Peter spent time in his early career in commercial roles in sales and account management.

Since moving into IT technical roles and later into senior management, this experience has helped him become a commercially strong leader. He has worked on leadership teams in businesses in numerous international markets, in various stages of growth and maturity, including private equity, high growth, and multinational environments, frequently partnering with start-ups to infuse new capabilities into organisations.

Peter has driven large scale programmes and delivered industry leading digital consumer experiences and products to market across a variety of industries such as gambling and hospitality.

Peter is a graduate from the University of Wales and of the IT Leadership Programme from the Cranfield School of Management.

https://www.linkedin.com/in/peterblower/

@peteblower

CIO Global

The Power of One, Going Global

Kevin Robins

Introduction

People often ask me what it is like to be a CIO/CTO in a global organisation. The short answer is it is not easy but when it is done right it can be very rewarding for the individual and very beneficial for the organisation. More and more these days there is a desire to go global, both business and IT. The newer organisations start with global in mind but for organisations that have been around for many years it is difficult as they have been built on bespoke legacy infrastructure and applications.

Previously global meant having a presence in many different countries with each country processing in different ways. Today going global means a lot more than this; it means having integrated systems; globally aligned processes and a workforce that operates not only in their home country but has full system access to operate in other countries. It means common system builds; an integrated network; common software base and patching. It also provides the opportunity to consolidate Data Centres and hopefully applications. I say hopefully as legacy applications are often country specific and closely coupled with clients. Whilst many companies are striving for global applications most companies with a legacy base have a lot of work to do to achieve this.

Stakeholder Engagement

Where do you start? I start with building relationships on many levels. First it is important to get the key stakeholders aligned i.e., CEO, CFO, COO. I have heard it said that the process of going global is like changing the engine in flight. The top team need to be fully on-board as there may be some turbulence on the way.

Next, it is important to get the local country General Managers engaged. It is hard for them to comprehend. Historically before organisations started to go global the General Manager was king of his kingdom. They ruled everything and had legal responsibility. Letting go is hard for them and time needs to be spent sharing the benefits of globalisation. Benefits include lower running costs; improved speed to market and access to a much wider talent pool. Even so letting go is still hard and the General Manager often feels that his or her role is being diminished.

Building the team

The next natural step in the relationship path is working with the local IT leads and with their teams. Some IT leads will never be able to make the transition. They feel that they will lose too much. The open minded and positive attitude ones will see the global opportunities that are opening up for them and a wonderful chance to enhance their career and become a global player. In a previous role I had one manager who did exactly this and within a year had a global team and was promoted to Vice President, something that would never have happened if he was just managing his own country. The teams themselves will be nervous of what this might mean for them. Going fully global gives the opportunity to reduce headcount in expensive locations but most switched on technicians and developers welcome the opportunity to be part of a wider team as it provides opportunity to expand their knowledge.

Defining the strategy and best practice

Strategy is the important factor that underpins globalisation. It needs to be built on a sound base otherwise it will not work. The way I have introduced it in the past is to look for some quick wins around processes and technology. For example, every country runs projects; operates change control; runs incidents; has development methodology; manages budgets. The result of these functions is the same but often there are many different ways of getting there. What I have done is to look for best practice and then deploy that best practice globally. I don't mind where that best practice originates. I once sat in on a night shift in Australia during a major change weekend. I saw the best *Post Implementation Review* process that I had ever seen. All home grown. I took this process and rolled it out across all countries. There is no commercial advantage to an organisation doing the same thing different ways.

Once the right team leads are established I always try to bring them all together for a few days and then have weekly team meetings with them. I know there is a time zone challenge but good willed people are happy to start early or stay late. The benefits are huge as they share best practice and bounce ideas off each other. It's amazing when you see that the same job is being done in many locations and one team expert shares experiences that save hours of work for the other team members. Once the processes are in place I nominate a lead to oversee that process globally and be the centre of excellence. This person will also ensure that we don't deviate from the agreed position.

Functional roles

Once the teams are starting to form around the technologies I then develop technology practices with a technology lead. I am looking for good people across all locations.

These practices include Project Managers. Business Analysts; Developers; Testers; Network Technicians; Infrastructure Developers.

Being part of a wider practice has huge advantages for the organisation and the individual. From an organisations perspective pooling people of the same skillset gives much more flexibility in terms of resourcing. For example; if a country has some major development work going on, then the chances are that the teams in that country will be really stretched. Being able to call on resources from around the world eases the burden. It enables development to start earlier and the delivery time to be shortened. It also allows a *'follow the sun approach'* for support.

I once had a major urgent development in Brazil but not the skills or people locally to do the work. I did however have skills and capacity in one of my Eastern Europe countries. For the cost of flights and hotels the development was delivered on time and to a high standard and the crisis was averted. Not only was the company very happy but the individuals liked the opportunity to travel and take part in the cultural exchange.

Putting the Infrastructure in place

To support and facilitate this global working requires a good and sound infrastructure base. I have found that it is easier to make progress on the infrastructure side than it is on the application side only for the reason that most of the time it is client independent. Most companies are working towards a global backbone network so that all countries can connect. The next step is then to allow access to systems from another country. There is some upfront investment needed in areas of Security and Active Directories. Also some countries will initially push back around access to Data Across Borders, I have found Germany and Poland to be the hardest two but even these are possible with some carefully written data access rules and local team members onsite to access the personal data. Once the *'plumbing'* is in place then the global team can start operating.

Cost Savings

The next area of quick wins with big cost savings is that of Infrastructure builds. A single software stack i.e. for windows, built in one location and propagated everywhere has to be a winner. It requires one development team and one support team. This is a cost saver in terms of time and money. It allows the other team members to work on other projects. It also makes applying patching worldwide so much easier.

Not only is a single build beneficial there is also another huge win. One build allows for a reduction in the number of third party software products. A common software stack means many software products can be retired and expensive maintenance stopped. When the number of third party products is added up globally it is not uncommon to find over 2000 different products. Most companies can run their systems on 10% of this number. Admittedly some of these products are harder to retire than others but it is still a big prize to go for and will help fund other aspects of the programme.

Improving Service

Another area to benefit from globalisation is that of service. Building the 'follow the sun' model means that teams working a day shift can take the lion share of the work. It doesn't mean that nightshifts disappear as there is always a local presence required but it does reduce them and the number of out of hours calls. Having all of the global systems being monitored and producing alerts from common products is very advantageous as it allows companies to build a global dashboard. Running common processes also reduces the complexity of running the operation and allows for much easier reporting. It enables global SLA's. The role of Operations is becoming very specialised and having a truly global function is extremely beneficial.

The Applications

By far the hardest area to globalise are the applications themselves. The applications can be split into client and internal. For client applications, each country has developed its client legacy application functionality with its clients. Data is often exchanged between clients and the host organisation. Whilst in many cases the same application is repeated across countries and clients it is done in many different ways. These are our legacy applications. Getting clients to change in the short term is difficult but a global product roadmap that can be implemented over time does work and clients will migrate across. Some wise clients may ask for a cost reduction as they know that your operating costs are being reduced!

There are always opportunities for internal systems i.e., HR and Finance to be consolidated into one global system and many companies are doing this. This in itself can create many benefits such as a single view of the customer and of the employees. The Finance team also benefit as it makes it much easier to roll up month and year end results into region then global. The development of both internal and client applications provides the IT team with endless opportunities to work closer with the business.

Marketing Ourselves

One aspect of our job that IT folks are very poor at is marketing our successes. The IT logical mind expects projects to go live and work as designed. Once one project is delivered we are already looking at our next project. I think it is very important that we break down our work into quick wins, share successes with the business and market across the organisation what we have done. Success breeds success and builds momentum. There will be some dark days when things don't always go as planned but having successes in the bank helps. It also shows the stakeholders and the business teams what they are getting in return for their investment. I have also found that most developers are not motivated by money on a day to day basis and an opportunity to share a success and receive a thank you goes a long way.

Going global is not an easy thing to do. It takes a sound vision; strong leadership; good stakeholder support; drive and flawless execution. There will be many wins and some setbacks along the way but the prize is huge and worth going for. Once the teams come on board momentum builds. For some people, the journey is not for them. They will leave the organisation.

For others, it is a stepping-stone to a bigger and wider career.

Communication

I will end with what I think is the most important success factor of all and that is communication.

As a leader you need to communicate, communicate and then communicate again. Once you reach the point that you feel you can communicate no more then I think it is probably a safe assumption that no more than 50% of the teams will have heard and really understood the message.

All that remains is for me to wish you good luck and a safe journey!

About Kevin Robins

Kevin Robins is an experienced CIO/CTO who has worked across the Banking, Retail and Payments industries; and has main board experience.

Kevin has also worked for *IBM* where he led teams across Retail Banking in the UK.

Kevin has over 30 years' experience of leading global transformations and consolidations.

Kevin has taken IT teams that have been operating in silos across numerous countries and brought them together into global functional teams operating on a matrix basis.

Kevin specialises in large change programmes that have delivered financial and productivity benefits for a number of organisations.

Kevin holds a Management MBA which was gained with Distinction and has recently been appointed as global CIO for *Sage*.

https://www.linkedin.com/in/kevin-robins-a701241/

CIO Career Path

The Start-up CIO

Ken Towning

I've worked in a few start-ups now but I am sharing the experience of my first, where most of the questions you should ask, should have been asked and answered too. My aim is to furnish you with key questions that need answers before and during your Start-Up tenure in order for you to concentrate on what is important.

I'd been in IT for 27 years, starting from the lowest rung as a Trainee PC Support Analyst working my way up to CIO. I loved every job in that time for different reasons and was now sitting comfortably financially too. I wanted to try something different and so joined a Start-up business where earnings would be lower than usual but I would have a stake (equity) in the company instead. When I say less, I really mean less than half my previous salary.

Looking back, it was a bigger risk than I realised before joining or even during the first year. So, before you make the leap, make sure you can afford it should the equity not materialise.

According to UK government statistics in 2016, only 60% of start-up businesses exist after five years. This figure includes start-ups that are bought or consumed by other businesses so 40% of business fail altogether. *(Source: Office For National Statistics, www.ons.gov.uk.)*

What took me by surprise was that the business could be sold and even as a shareholder or option holder pay-outs are not guaranteed. Do your homework on the equity being offered and the conditions under which they will be paid out.

The business was a four-year-old 'start-up', a retail company with a niche proposition, to sell premium and luxury goods at a discount in a series of flash sales. Within days it felt like it was my business but then again, it was, or at least in part. The idea of having equity attached to the value of the company was a real motivator. IT was at the core of this online-only business helping to grow it to £80m revenue so far and I was on the Exec Board influencing anything from marketing to logistics. It felt like I had joined a small family on the Exec Board, all with a say, though not everyone saw eye to eye, we all had the same goal; to grow the business. I was about to find out that CIO would not be the only role I would be fulfilling in this small business, not that this was ever discussed before I joined. It is important to identify what other roles are not filled and therefore you might be expected to perform them such as leading on HR or Operations issues.

The plan was to drive the business towards £250m revenue in two to three years so I provided blood, sweat and tears along with everyone else. It was weird though, an online-only business with just six IT staff yet over 120 in total. The six included all disciplines of IT including the development team of two! Lean wasn't the word. Generally, start-ups don't pay well and the IT staff were inexperienced and ill-trained something I only found out after accepting the role. Particularly with start-ups, you must identify what IT organisation structure, size, skills and experience are your responsibility.

I agreed to join because there was a clear vision, a new CEO and fresh investment from Venture Capitalists. This is vital for any new role. These three things declare a serious objective and the means to get there.

It's important to know what the promises are to the investors, Board and staff. On joining I was told a new, off the shelf, ecommerce system was being implemented to replace a bespoke and home-grown system written by a genius developer. It was a nightmare, twice we tried to go live, working through the night to complete the change-over and twice it failed to run fast enough, even on cloud services. I had missed my own instinct to challenge the process that determined this was the right ecommerce system for the job because it was a done deal before I arrived. Worse, I also knew we were not addressing the core issues of the business either. The ecommerce side of things was relatively stable. However, tracking customer orders and the supply chain was terrible. The *Enterprise Resource Planning* system was a well-known one but it had lots of custom code that repeatedly failed and gave us no insight relating to the progress of an order for a customer. Returns and refunds were not only very high but we couldn't track them properly either. It was a mess, how we could even reliably report revenue each month was a mystery and that was the point, it was mostly guess work.

After the two front-end website launch failures, the conversations on our Exec Board were getting fractious and even worse with the Investment Board. I was hauled in front of the Investment Board to explain the failures. The new system simply was not built with flash sales in mind. It was a standard commerce system not designed to handle 50 new promotions with anything up to 200 new products and the lapsing of 50 old promotions in one day. It was the merchandising side that really failed; copy, text and images for the all the products in each new promotion were taking forever to be loaded, manipulated and presented. These slow processes directly impacted the performance of the website for customers too. The software partner was working really hard to try and fix things but it was always down to their own two gurus who were tired, running out of ideas and spread thinly across a number of clients, many of whom were larger than us and wanted simple updates to their own systems. Our requirements were more than pushing the boundary of their core product and so the new system was becoming bespoke, again.

Suddenly, our VCs needed project and business progress reports on a weekly basis. This was a business that had managed to get through the many difficult early 'start-up' phases.   It is also necessary to understand what round of investment the business is in, as this will indicate the start-up stage.

The founders had taken the business through 'finding a problem', 'finding a solution', 'finding the backing', 'finding the product', 'finding the market', 'finding the channel' and even 'finding more backing' for expansion. This just left expanding the business stage and then the 'finding a suitable exit' stage

We were failing to expand, worse we were contracting. By now, existing customers were frustrated with the website being messed with as well the poor post-order customer experience. A double whammy.

I took more control of IT now reverting to solving small issues in the incumbent ecommerce system to help it steer us through peak trading periods. One morning the data guy who reported to the CEO, an awkward chap for most colleagues but I respected his capability nonetheless, came to me and told me he needed more power in his data warehouse, but not for reporting, he believed he could help inform customers and ourselves with more information from the DWH.

We discussed categorisation of customers, personalisation of webpages and even improving the tracking information provided to customers. I ordered the upgrade immediately. The IT team and the data analyst wrote a personalised section for every logged in customer with recommendations, recent purchases and order tracking interface in less than four weeks. It was amazing.

We could see the uplifts in customer interest and purchases on the site within days.

Meanwhile, we needed to be careful with cash now so we reduced our business marketing spend. This caused a wave of concern amongst the employees and we had to manage that carefully as a Board over the coming months. Customer acquisition was down as a result of less marketing and so retaining and encouraging existing customers was then more important than ever. We could only do this by improving post-sale experience by messaging customers the progress of orders speedily and accurately. I hired a new ERP specialist, he was a god-send. Slowly we overhauled the bespoke code in the ERP to now track customer and supplier orders properly, good data was now arriving in the DWH and we could now see some stability in existing customer numbers and their order behaviours.

Our main marketing lifeline was now the daily email campaigns and we managed to personalise these too, helping us to at least hold on to existing numbers for customers and orders. This wasn't enough, something else needed to change as operating costs were too high and we had too many staff supporting marketing and merchandising.

Then came the shattering news.

The VCs had decided to back a similar company in addition to retreating from future funding promises. We had to look for new investors or be bought earlier than planned. Either way it meant we had to reduce the operating costs as growth without marketing funding would be impossible and the business still had no single month of operating profit.

We made roles redundant and this is when you realise that in a start-up you are more than a CIO. I was now helping to lead on people issues across the business as well logistics. It was an uncomfortable time and messy with people at different stages of their careers and differing points of views.

After just a few months we hit our first monthly operating profit. I attended countless meetings with potential investors and buyers all the time improving both the backend and front-end systems.

We launched a clearance site, with fast tracked delivery times, something that seemed impossible when I started, we were emailing customers with progress updates that were accurate and we managed to move the core systems to the cloud making them more resilient, scalable and high performing.

However, one of the main investors, a VC, decided the similar business should purchase our business as it had more 'assets' even though it was operating at a greater loss and so the transaction happened. It was gutting. I, with others, was kept on the usual retainer for six months. The business was sold under-value due to the lack of revenue growth and general belief in the potential. Those of us with equity holdings did not benefit from the sale, it was a sore time after two years of really hard graft, I literally had not been so consumed at work like that before.

So, what are the three main things to expect when you become a CIO of a start-up.

- You are not just a CIO, more than likely you oversee other areas too, like People and Logistics.

- You will need to get your hands dirty, there are not enough people and there is not enough money to farm all the jobs out.

- You won't be paid at the value you give yourself and nor should you bank on equity returns.

Right, now you know what to expect, what is expected of you?

First of all, and it goes without saying, but I will anyway – bring solutions, not problems. It is a mindset and a behaviour that I had every day. It breaks barriers, reverberates and encourages others and provides a much greater level of personal satisfaction. In a start-up it helps if you are the sort of CIO that is fascinated by most things, helping to solve all problems not just technical ones.

You will need to be both patient as there is a lack of money and talent, and resilient as the problems keep on coming. You need to be persistent, not everything will work first time and the last trait required is being innovative. Now this doesn't have to take the form of something like inventing the next blockchain, it can be something as simple as applying previous experience to this new business.

Start-ups are not for the faint-hearted!

Me? I am on my fourth Start-up now so it cannot be all bad!

About Ken Towning

In a career spanning 30 years, Ken has loved the variety of working in many organisations differing in size, industry and location. Ken's CIO roles have been just as diverse from working in innovative Start-ups to international corporates looking to transform. Ken is curious about all businesses and commercially focussed.

Ken worked across many disciplines in IT including project management, software development and infrastructure and has recently been overseeing IoT, blockchain and AI projects. Ken remains committed to helping all types of companies harness digital change.

After starting as Trainee PC Support Analyst in *Willis Towers Watson,* Ken has worked in several delivery, strategy and executive roles in *British American Tobacco, British Telecom, Sainsburys, Marks and Spencer, Argos* and *TalkTalk* and smaller Start-up companies such as *Entier, ACHICA* and *ManagedSelf.*

Ken was a not-for-profit Board member of a semi-professional football club having served as Treasurer, Vice Chairman and Chairman after many years as a coach.

Ken sits on the Advisory Board of *Sullivan & Stanley* and has recently completed a series of Non-Executive Board member courses.

Ken is a family man and enjoys spending as much time as possible with his wonderful wife Maria and children, Charlie, Billy and Grace.

www.linkedin.com/in/ken-towning

@primeInterim

My first CIO Gig

Paul Hobbs

My CIO Calling

I was in my tenth year at a FTSE 100 International Public-Sector Outsourcing provider that had grown from £1 billion to over £4 billion turnover and grown to employ 100,000 staff in my time there. I had spent my first five years leading customer bids and implementing customer contracts and the last five years in the Group CIO team transforming the business from a collection of 800 autonomously run contracts, into a modern business powered by connected Enterprise systems, IT services and off-shore administration and processing centres.

I was the IT Services Director reporting to the CIO, responsible for the efficiency and effectiveness of IT Services across the group.

The CIO, although not a technologist by training, was a smart, inspirational leader who understood big picture IT and commanded respect right across the business, I enjoyed working for him, had learned a lot from him and had played my part in delivering a massive transformation agenda, but something was missing.

I missed the buzz of winning and implementing customer contracts, I had moved too far from the end customer and I also realised that I felt ready to be a CIO in my own right. So, when a head hunter called with what sounded like a great opportunity, I was open to listening.

The CIO Opportunity

The company that had the open CIO position was a much smaller outfit with a £60 million turnover and 2500 staff across six countries with 70% of the business in the UK. It specialised in what was called 'Welfare to Work' which meant contracting to governments and helping the long term unemployed back into sustainable employment.

I went to meet the head hunter and he put me forward to a panel interview in which I had to do a presentation on what my 100-day plan would be. On the panel was the exiting CIO who was based in Australia and did not want to move to the UK so was leaving, the European CEO and the UK CEO.

I wanted the interview to be a two-way process, not only did I want to give a good account of myself but I also wanted to find out if these guys on the opposite side of the table were people that I wanted to work with so I asked a number of questions about culture and their aspirations for the business.

What I found out was that the UK CEO had a fantastic vision for how he wanted to take this relatively small business and transform it into the number one 'Welfare to Work' provider in the UK by making it the highest performing organisation with the lowest costs. He explained that the *Department of Work and Pensions* (DWP) was just about to release a tender for a new contract called the Work Programme (WP) that was going to be the vehicle upon which his strategy was going to be delivered. We discussed and brainstormed how technology could play a massive role in delivering this vision and I was hooked.

Hitting the Ground Running

Shortly after I started in September 2010 it was announced that the WP bid was being issued in two months' time, with bid submission two months after that, preferred bidder two months after that and go-live two months after that. As the WP was the overriding business priority, all other activity was to be minimised or put on hold. My job for the next eight months was to lead the technology elements of the plan necessary to bid, win and deliver the WP.

Assessing for Growth

My initial assessment of IT in the company was that if it wanted to continue as it was then the IT set up was perfectly adequate. But as we wanted to become the Number One player in the Industry the organisation was going to have to grow by 3 or 4 times in size and become much more efficient. It is against this context that I assessed IT's fitness for the future as follows:

- The IT team was small at 17 members but my impression was that there was some excellent people in it and that I could build a delivery strategy around them.

- The Email system was not fit for purpose for the new scale and in need of upgrade.

- The Finance system replacement project was already in-train and would need to be implemented in the middle of the WP transformation programme, as the project was too advanced to be put on hold.

- The Case Management System (CMS) being used had very limited functionality with no work flow, no client self-help portal and would need substantial development and testing to be scaled as was required, if we stayed with it.

- There were two data centres, one in Paris and one in London, both had grown organically with cabinets spread over multiple floors in Tier 3 facilities and a mass of wires connecting the cabinets. The hardware in the data centres was end of life.

As we would be operating at the UK Government 'Official' security level, physical Data Centres in the UK were going to be required (at that time in 2010) for the WP contract.

- End User Devices (PC's, Multi-Functional Devices etc) were all end of life and out of contract.

- Telecoms (WAN & VoIP) had grown organically and never been competed commercially and as we were going to open 80-120 new offices; existing lines were mostly in the wrong locations, so now was a perfect time to do a market test.

So, the good news was that we had the basis of a good team and that there were not many commercial or technical constraints to the way forward, but equally, there was a lot of work to do to be ready in eight months, with no certainty of what or where we had won contracts until two months before go-live.

Thinking and Planning My Way Through The Issues

Planning is one of my core skills, so as I didn't have access to a programme planner at the time, I set about putting together a high-level plan to deliver all the different technology programme streams and then to use it to get business buy-in to my plan.

One issue that I anticipated was that we would need to start activities and start spending money before we knew what contracts we had won.

The trick was going to be to delay spending as long as possible and to do that I had to demonstrate when money needed to be spent by drawing out the programme plan with all its programme streams, activity timings and the interdependencies between the different activities on the different programme streams.

The plan showed that there were seven commercial procurements to be conducted and supply contracts to be negotiated.

I presented the high-level programme plan together with a resourcing plan and a phased spending plan and received authority to proceed, from the Board.

As I have mentioned there were some excellent people in the IT team that understood the business inside-out so my strategy was to target these people at the tasks that most needed their expert domain knowledge and bring in resources to work alongside them on the other more generic tasks that they had previously performed and could oversee with little effort.

Initial Priorities

The high-level programme plan highlighted that we needed to get on with certain infrastructure streams without delay, so that the team could move onto other 'dependent' streams later.

Priorities for imminent start were:

- Replacing the email system
- Building a model office
- Designing and building one data centre from which we could start operations

The business exec had bought into the risk assessment that showed that starting operations with only one data centre represented a lower risk than trying to design and build a two data centre operation in the time before go-live.

Up-Scaling and Designing the Operating Model

I also brought in a trusted boutique Telecoms procurement consultancy to take on the task of procuring the most cost-effective data and voice telecoms networks for our requirements as I had no-one else that could do that to the level of quality that they could deliver.

To scale up the team quickly I had access to technical staff from a top management consultancy firm at 'mate's rates' so I quickly got in good quality trusted staff to scale the team as described above.

One of the advantages of using these guys was that they had a lot of experience of process design and process automation. Through a series of cross-functional workshops involving the senior leadership team, key staff and the management consultants, the vision for the new ways of operating were drawn out. This vision was then broken down into lower level processes and the companies new operating model had now been completely re-engineered to make it more efficient and effective for the new WP contract.

Finding the Right Solution

Once we had the new Operating Model we were able to start work on the CMS stream of the technology programme. We needed a functionally rich solution that was field proven and that had a very high probability of being delivered in time for operational training before the go-live date.

We needed to get business case approval for this solution before the bid was submitted both because it was a significant cost line in the bid but also because it would not be ready in time if we did not start this stream at least six months before go-live.

Within two weeks of the operating model being finalised we had a set of 300 functional and 100 non-functional requirements for the CMS and we had a short list of potential solutions who were interested in tendering for it, including the incumbent.

We ran the Request For Proposal (RFP) process in three weeks and did our due diligence on each solution so that when the CMS business case was presented for sign off, we had confidence that the recommended solution was deliverable within the available timescale and would pass the required penetration tests, and the new supplier was given *'Preferred Bidder'* status until contracts were agreed and signed.

Once the business case for the CMS was signed off we had 16 weeks to deliver the solution into the training environment for operator training. To do this we constructed a cross functional project team, including the CMS suppliers team members, to work using the Agile methodology to deliver the solution, ensuring that all high priority functionality was delivered up front to de-risk the project as much as possible.

Submitting the Bid

When we submitted the WP bid we also had to submit a *'Security Plan'* with it that detailed how our solution would conform to *ISO27001* and the Governments *'Official'* security standard.

Submitting the bid was a big milestone, but there was no time to rest, as the next weekend we were due to go-live in our new data centre. Our supplier had created a secure, caged ten cabinet suite for us with the required power and cooling for less than we had been paying for the distributed cabinets that we had used before.

The Infrastructure guys had designed the data centre, run a competition for the required networking and hosting hardware, and configured, installed and tested all the new kit.

Over that weekend, kit that was being reused was moved, the new configurations applied and a holistic set of tests conducted to ensure that everything would be working on Monday morning.

When Monday came around we had full support on hand, but no-one even noticed that we had moved the data centre, except for nearly everything being a lot faster.

The Model Office was a great success, with fantastic user feedback and it put us in a great position to roll out offices in a standard build set up, with minimal on-site infrastructure, once we knew where we needed offices.

Contract Announcement

DWP announced their *Preferred Bidder* and of the 41 contracts that they were letting we had won the largest seven giving us a leading 24% market share, twice as big as the second place provider. The whole company celebrated in Shoreditch that night, had the weekend off, and then got stuck into rollout planning.

Rolling our Sleeves Up

The weeks to go-live were intense but we managed to complete all the Customer and Supplier commercial negotiations and contract sign off's and keep all the plates spinning for all the programme streams required for go-live.

Before we were allowed to go-live we had to conduct and pass a holistic set of Penetration tests. We planned enough time for one set of re-tests in case we did not pass them all first time and in the event only needed to redo two of the tests, which we passed with 3 days to spare before go-live.

We received 1000 client referrals electronically from DWP on go-live day and they all flowed through our system and were successfully processed. All the hard work had paid off.

What a Ride, What a Result

My first eight months being a CIO had been a whirlwind of activity, we had delivered a major Transformation Programme on time and to budget.

I had changed my career path to become a CIO and I had enjoyed every minute of it. We had achieved something special because everyone in the company had pulled together and worked as one team and delivered a great result.

We were to go on to become the top performing provider in all seven of the areas that we operated in and help 500,000 of the most disadvantaged members of society make a positive change to their lives and get back into sustainable employment.

About Paul Hobbs

Paul Hobbs is an innovative, inspiring and delivery focused technology leader who creates game changing technology solutions, in collaboration with stakeholders. Achieved by having the experience and judgement to know what good looks like, by inspiring teams to perform and by always thinking clearly under pressure. For 22 years Paul has been leading IT/ Digital strategy, IT/Digital Transformations and IT Operations and was awarded a *Queen's Award* for *Industry for Innovation* for one of his early Transformations.

Paul trained in Engineer & Management and Operational Research before starting his career as a Product Planner at *Rover*. He then progressed through Operational Consultancy, Logistics management and Business Programmes before directing IT Organisations and Programmes in International Business Services, providing outsourced Services to both the public and private sectors.

Paul has significant experience in complex international and domestic stakeholder engagement, large scale programme management, process automation and application modernisation, digital marketing, data analytics and artificial intelligence robotics, supplier contracting and complex contract negotiation, outsourcing, near shoring and off-shoring, IT Infrastructure, Security, Cloud and Omni Channel.

www.linkedin.com/in/paul-hobbs-63b49b13

The Journey to Investor CIO

Malcolm Lambell

My story starts from the end of my permanent career through to my time as an Interim and then my portfolio career as an 'Investor CIO and Advisor.'

I was a permanent CIO for over 24 years and mostly I thoroughly enjoyed it. However, I must admit that the last seven years firstly, as an Interim and then transitioning into a true investor/entrepreneur has been more fun, more satisfying and financially more rewarding.

I will start by going back to my last permanent CIO role.

The 'Permanent' Phase

It was August 2010 - I had been working at the *Royal Bank of Scotland* in multiple con-current roles as CIO, CTO and Global Programme Director. I ran India and at the peak I had 2,500 employees in two continents. It wasn't fun though; the banking crisis had hit hard and the bank, along with many financial institutions, was effectively bankrupt. To be honest it was embarrassing working in such an arrogant organisation during a global financial disaster that it had helped happen. I am sure you will remember the whole story unfolding in the media.

I managed to engineer a 'good leaver' exit and left with a bit of a payoff and some potentially precious employee options. (I just missed them being worth £50,000 by about three months.)

Being out of work held no fears for me. Due to the ongoing rationalisation in the financial services industry the companies I worked for were often being acquired.

Having been made redundant a few times, I found that I always seemed to get a better job almost straightaway. In fact, I seemed to develop a sixth sense for seeing it coming and often finished on a Friday with one company (and a good redundancy package) and started with another on the Monday!

As I left *RBS* I wondered if I really wanted another permanent CIO role. I felt I needed a new challenge.

I think CIOs forget how much value they are sitting on. I had delivered eight significant transformation programmes in my permanent career and I had a great reputation for coming up with creative solutions. Like all successful CIOs I had developed good skills in the areas of leadership, supplier management, finance, stakeholder engagement and technology whilst being able to operate at strategic, tactical and operational levels.

I had been thinking about setting up my own business for a while and then I had a 'defining moment'. I met with a head-hunter I had known for many years, she said go Interim – you will love it! It was the push I needed!

The 'Early Interim' Phase

I did a lot of research on being an Interim. Most of my contacts were head-hunters so I had to completely refocus my network on agencies who could find me work or colleagues who may need me to work for them.

I decided to really invest in getting to know the agents. I contacted them and after they had seen my CV many said pop in for coffee. I made sure I met as many as possible, in fact I think I spent about £3,000 in travel costs in three months.

I knew that this would be a good investment and I soon got to know the agents very well. I treated every meeting like an interview, selling what I had achieved and what I could do. Interestingly, I was offered two good contracts in the first two weeks. Later, as an established Interim, I found out that the agents would monitor the end date of my contracts so they could be first to put me out on my next 'gig.'

In the early days, I branded myself as 'Programme Director and IT Executive'. The reason was I didn't think there would be many good Interim IT Executive leadership roles. I could not have been more wrong.

A few of my colleagues started by setting up a consultancy. I didn't want to do that, I decided to set up my business (Transformation Partners) to focus on Interim assignments with consulting in mind for the future.

It's funny when Pauline (my wife) and I raised our first invoice it was massively satisfying. I felt the same when our first set of company accounts came through, it was so strange depreciating a laptop at £150 a year, I had been used to seeing depreciation of £30m a year in my permanent CIO roles!

My first 'gig' was with Vertex Financial Services (business process outsourcer) based in Cheltenham. The role was Head of Applications and I was to close the Life and Pensions business line. I quite liked the idea of working 'service side' rather than 'client' side. The role also entailed selling which was interesting.

When I started I had two major shocks. Firstly, everyone was so friendly and treated me with real respect (very different from RBS). Secondly, I was surprised by how much I was listened to.

I soon learned that Interims have a lot more 'power' than permanent employees because they are not interested in a career with the client so they are a lot less threatening to their peers. Additionally, they are often employed to deliver something specific so they can act outside the politics and therefore be very effective.

All this was a massive surprise to me. I really hadn't expected it and I really loved it.

The work was very rewarding and I worked with some very talented people. I ended up doing three brilliant roles: *Vertex* (18 months,) *Bupa* (three years) and *XL Catlin* (two years).

I think it is quite unusual for an Interim to have so many long 'gigs.' However, I never tried to unnecessarily extend a contract and never asked for a rate increase at contract extension and made that a key part of my Interim 'brand.'

The 'Interim Plus' Phase

As part of my Interim business and alongside my Interim work, I decided to deliver workshops and consulting assignments. I also built three management games which I used in my assignments. I sold one of the games for £3,000! They were great fun to build and I really enjoyed testing them out with my family.

Adding Mentoring and Outplacement

I had delivered quite a bit of mentoring in my permanent roles and to be honest I enjoyed working with talented colleagues who wanted to grow their career and skills. I felt I needed some work which was more 'nurturing,' rather than just raw delivery.

So, alongside my Interim roles I started to sell mentoring as part of my services to corporate clients and billed them by the hour. Financially it was a bit of a disaster. I felt I had to chase them to get any time and with travel it really wasn't worth doing. I changed the hourly billing to a yearly fee of £3,500. It's a successful and very content rich offering and is targeted at CIOs and CIO's direct reports.

Then something quite unexpected happened.

I was contacted by a couple of people I knew who were out of work and wanted some of my contacts to help them find a job. I am always happy to help, but I suggested we turn it into a commercial arrangement and make it a proper outplacement service.

I would coach them on their CV, interview skills, set up trial interviews, open my network to them and generally support the process. Twenty clients later, I have a 95% success record (one is in progress) and my most successful outcome is a client who achieved a £400,000 package. I charge £1,500 to start working with them and £2,000 when they have a role, sharing the risk with the client seems to work well.

Starting the Investor Phase

As I progressed my Interim career, I thought about how I would want to work in the future. I had been working for over 40 years, I knew I didn't want to finish working, but I didn't want to work five days a week doing the same job.

I started to think about new ventures. I felt I wanted to set up a business that could potentially be sold in say 10 years. Transformation Partners, like most businesses run by Interims, has no resale value. The Interim is the business and as such there are no assets other than the cash in the bank.

I wanted to build something special. I focused on finding an opportunity with three key attributes. Firstly, a growing market with a technology connection. Secondly, that I could find someone very talented to run it (I was not inclined to be the CEO myself). Thirdly, that I could afford to have some equity whist not risking too much of my personal capital.

Rivington Information Security

My chosen market became information security and I found a brilliant CEO who I had known for a long time and was someone I respected and trusted.

We met and started the planning process. The 'CEO designate' was very busy in his current role so I focused on the business plan. I am not an information security specialist and did a lot of research, both on information security and setting up businesses from scratch. Together we ended up with a quality 50-page business plan.

The hardest thing was finding a name; in the end we called it Rivington Information Security, named after a steak restaurant in Dubai!

Next was funding. I was not allowed to approach investors without warning them formally of the risks of a start-up business and ensuring that they had sufficient wealth to accept the risk. I found a Government supported scheme called *SEIS (Seed Enterprise Investment Scheme)* and *EIS (Enterprise Investment Scheme)* which enables an investor to invest and receive 50% tax relief for SEIS and 30% for EIS.

A huge thank you to Simon Crookston of Crowe Clark Whitehill and Nick Gabay of *Thomson Snell and Partners* who helped to lead us through the complex rules and conditions associated with these schemes.

When I started to approach investors (I was personally only allowed 30% of the equity due to the scheme rules) I found people were very interested. However even though I have a good network I got to the point where 20% of the equity remained unsold. Then I met with my IFA to talk about my finances and in passing he said he would take 10%. That convinced a couple of other investors and we were there! I raised £450,000 through ten investors.

We have been in business for almost three years and as I write this we have three prestige clients (our first being the *Bank of England*) and have another three or four new clients in the pipeline, plus some very strong strategic relationships with key product partners. We are profitable and have just recruited a Sales Director as part of our growth plan.

When we started we agreed that we would ensure that all our work was reference-able and of the highest quality, we wanted to take a long-term view of the business and wanted to build something special. We have very strong business principles. For instance, we are more likely to reward our team for great client feedback rather than sales.

We have just had our second employee conference and I must say there is nothing more rewarding as being in a conference with your team designing the future of the business and seeing all your ideas coming to fruition. Personally, seeing the business plan come to life is incredible and is like opening a children's pop-up book.

It's been massively rewarding. As I type I am in the process of shutting down Transformation Partners (my Interim limited company) and focussing on being a CIO Investor and Advisor.

In Summary

My message to CIOs coming to the end of their permanent career ...

The world is your oyster ... Interim work, NED, setting up companies ... you have the skills so go for it!

About Malcolm Lambell

Malcolm has had a long career in IT Executive roles leading significant business and technology transformation.

His most recent permanent role was as CIO, CTO and Global Programme Director at the *Royal Bank of Scotland* where he managed a team of 2,500 across two continents.

Previously he worked for the *Cheltenham and Gloucester Building Society, TSB, Prudential, AXA PPP Healthcare, Woolwich, Lloyds Group* and *HBOS*.

In 2010 he decided to become a 'career' Interim. He set up Transformation Partners which delivered Interims, consulting and mentoring. His Interim assignments were: *Vertex Financial Services, Bupa* and *XL Catlin*.

In 2014, inspired by his success with Transformation Parters he founded *Rivington Information Security Limited*. Malcolm is the Executive Chairman of the business, which now has a number of prestigious clients and is building a strong reputation and brand.

Malcolm is a Non Executive and investor with *Pentagon Consulting Limited*.

In 2017 he closed *Transformation Partners* and brought his Interim career to an end in order to focus on his growing portfolio of interests. He is currently exploring other business ventures and NED roles.

Malcolm offers advisory services to CIOs and IT Executives seeking career moves.

malcolmg_lambell@hotmail.com

linkedin.com/in/malcolmlambell

www.rivingtoninformationsecurity.com

Ten Learnings for a Transformational CIO

Chris Michael

I stay very close to technology, because I'm a geek, and because it's moving so fast. Over the last 30 years, I've helped transform many great brands but what keeps me motivated is the knowledge that I'll learn more tomorrow.

Learning 1: Follow your passion, even if you have to break the rules.

I studied Mechanical Engineering at University because I loved solving problems. I wanted to design physical products and I believed it was important to know how stuff actually worked.

By the start of my final year I knew I didn't want to be an Engineer, but instead had developed a passion for business. A fellow student and I convinced the head of department to let us setup up a business as our final year project. I saw this as a way to complete my degree and also as an escape route to another career.

Learning 2: Solve a real user need.

The idea for our business was simple: to understand why so many talented Engineering students didn't want to follow a career in Engineering.

We ran a syndicated research programme across all Engineering courses in the UK, asking thousands of students what they were looking from an employer, and why they were avoiding a career in Engineering.

One key insight was that students thought Engineers were poorly paid, but didn't actually know how much they could earn. We convinced recruiters to provide that information to candidates. We then sold the results back to these employers.

Learning 3: Do something which stands out.

Later that year, we launched a publication, called Facts, which showcased Engineering employers.

Facts was transformational. It was exclusively designed for engineering students, it was independent, professionally written by a journalist, and it listed actual salaries.

Over the next three years, we expanded the user base, grew advertising revenue, drove down costs and started to make some money.

Learning 4: On-premise technology sucks.

In the early 90s recruiters stopped employing graduates so Facts suffered. I'd learnt how to publish journals straight out of a database, so I took these learnings on the road as an independent consultant and built database publishing systems for a number of publishers, including *Pearson, Emap* and *News International*.

By the mid 90's the world wide web started to take off, and my clients were asking me to help take their publications online, requiring me to build a business and employ people - developers with specific coding skills. By the end of the 90s I had two companies and employed ten developers.

My core business was building smart database driven web technologies.

My 'side' business was an ERP system for the creative industry, called Creative Office. It was very smart and did everything except make the tea: CRM, job/project management, timesheets, billing, purchasing, and full financial reporting. It had a great UX and people love using it. We had clients ranging from self-employed freelancers through to 200-person agencies.

But there were some problems.

Firstly, every client wanted something different and, over time, the code base became bloated with way too many custom features.

Secondly, super-fast broadband didn't exist yet. So that meant a lot of travelling to run demos, close deals, and provide support. Cloud computing wasn't mainstream and businesses didn't trust having their data on someone else's servers. The technology required installation on each company's network which drove costs up.

By 2000, I conceded this was not scalable, nor profitable. Now there are many cloud platforms, like *Salesforce* and *Xero*, which can scale and do a brilliant job cost effectively.

Learning 5: Don't try to do everything yourself.

Concentrating on my core business, I catered to Dot Com start-ups through to large global blue-chip brands.

The late 90s saw the birth and growth of digital agencies. Many became famous for building cool front-end experiences, typically in Adobe Flash. I took a different approach, building smart back-end systems which used data to drive and improve the end-to-end experience for users.

Then, in 2001, the dot com bubble burst and many of my smaller clients disappeared overnight, leaving *British Telecom (BT)* as my biggest client, via a direct marketing agency called *HHM*.

I knew I needed more clients like BT to grow, so I sold my business to *HHM* and joined them as Technology Director which turned out to be a very smart move. And over the next five years, we grew clients and revenue.

Learning 6: Data is essential to drive insight and action.

We became BT's digital agency, helping them launch broadband in the UK. We took pre-orders from customers via their phone number and email address. As and when exchanges reached a certain stage (e.g. announced, confirmed, enabled), the platform would send automated triggers out with a link to the order form. Of course, now you can do this all in *MailChimp* out of the box.

As well as running digital campaigns, we also designed and built content management systems and transactional platforms for clients such as *Amex, Ladbrokes* and *UKTV*.

Then in 2006, three other directors and I bought *HHM*, re-branded the business as *Crayon* and created a 'challenger' digital agency. While we retained BT, other clients wanted a bigger agency.

In 2009, we sold to *Hicklin Slade*, and I joined them as Technology and User Experience Director. Much like *HHM*, they were a direct marketing agency running digital campaigns for *Hicklin Slade's* existing clients (such as *Honda* and *Sony*).

We proceded to win over brands including *Axa, British Gas, DeBeers, Deutsche Bank, Laithwaites, Porsche* and *William Grant*. And we introduced a new level of rigour into collecting data, and dramatically improved the user experience for all of these clients.

For example, we introduced smart technology to drive conversions on BT.com. We used a mix of *Clicktale* and *Omniture* (now *Adobe Analytics*) to understand user behaviour, then ran a series of pilots with *Optimost, Maxymiser,* and *Test & Target* (now *Adobe Target*) to find the best platform and approach. The results were astounding, increasing conversions by 40%. BT then adopted the technology and processes to implement a programme of ongoing AB and Multivariate testing.

By 2011, I became a massive advocate of Advanced Analytics and Multivariate testing and used this to help *Direct Wines* (including their two main brands, *Laithwaites* and *Sunday Times Wine Club*) increase sales and profit by over 20% in the first six months.

Learning 7: Mobile > Desktop.

In 2012, we sold *Crayon* to a private equity firm who'd just bought *Karmarama,* an independent advertising agency; and this blended above the line creativity with data-driven technology.

As BT's retained digital agency, we focused on continual ongoing optimisation but started to notice something very interesting. Mobile traffic was growing rapidly but the experience was so terrible on a mobile device, that it was almost impossible to complete an order.

Making the whole of bt.com 'mobile friendly' became a priority but was not going to be easy nor cheap. We setup a targeted PPC campaign, which drove users to a mobile optimised microsite with a simplified user journey for a single product. Conversion jumped to 400% better than the non-optimised journey.

Extrapolating the expected growth rate of mobile traffic would deliver an annual revenue increase of £30-£60m.

And we knew if we did nothing, that this revenue would be lost. In order to simplify the user experience for smaller screens, we'd ruthlessly cut any content not deemed essential. And when we applied this approach to larger screens (laptops and desktops), we discovered overall conversions actually increased!

Over the next 12 months, we helped BT implement responsive mobile designs across all of their sites and converted many other clients' websites to mobile responsive designs too. Most sites you see today are mobile responsive, and have much less clutter.

Learning 8: Insourcing > Outsourcing.

Over the years, we'd helped many clients generate significant incremental revenue and profit. But there were a number of recurring issues. Clients often had terrible legacy technology, and were almost always at the mercy of a big, expensive system integrator. This limited the ability to getting, for example, a real time data feed, or integrating a transactional mobile app.

By mid 2014, I'd had enough of agency life and felt I could make a bigger difference focusing on one client.

I spent a year in Government, leading three digital teams at the Ministry of Justice. I was humbled by the passion and dedication of so many brilliant people, all solving very real problems and making a big difference to so many users. This was in stark contrast to the shocking behaviour of some of the incumbent systems integrators at the time.

I did what I could to expose bad practice, over charging and underperformance, saving millions of pounds of tax payers money.

In 2015, I was headhunted to build the global digital technology practice inside *Reckitt Benckiser (RB)*. *RB* had over 5000 websites, built by a multitude of different agencies, using many different technologies.

The plan was to get this into a single platform (based on *Hybris*) and then to enable this for ecommerce, so we could sell products direct to consumers online.

I started with a couple of specialist consultancies, and then setup new in-house business units in Warsaw and Amsterdam.

We migrated everything onto a single platform in AWS, and started to build out predictive models based on previous period sales, market data, social, search and even weather. The platform gave every sales person across the company the ability to measure real time granular sales versus targets. This enabled faster decision making and actions which increased sales. It also enabled more effective media spend based on predicted future sales. The platform was directly responsible for £100m incremental net revenue in the first year.

The key was a strong internal team. Having good partners is essential, but it is even more important to have internal capability. You get to understand much better what services you are buying, and you are much better placed to manage vendor and partner relationships too.

Learning 9: Employ people better than you.

By 2016, I left *RB* to join *Open Banking* as Head of Technology to build the API standards for banking in the UK. I knew a lot about implementing APIs to enable digital services on top of legacy systems, but knew less about payments.

Some leaders like to build big teams and manage big budgets but this is often not sustainable and works less well if you are looking to transform a business (or an entire industry).

Over the years, I've developed a simple approach to building teams. Having the right office is key. It needs to be in a location and have an environment where people like to spend time.

If you are stuck in a dull office with a toxic atmosphere, it is very hard to find and keep good people.

Sometimes you need to setup a new external office, and this is often cheaper and easier than getting the right space in an existing building. I then look to solve a single problem as quickly as possible. I identify the one or two key skills I need for this, and recruit the very best people I can. And I look for a mix of people inside the business and people I've worked with elsewhere before; each covering a range of skills.

Internal stakeholder support is vital. You can't get anything done without funding from the board. But just as important is having a strong HR partner, who can help you find the right people quickly, as speed is often key.

I particularly look for "T" or "π" (Pi) shaped people, who are subject matter experts in one or (preferably) two areas, but who have a good knowledge across many others. Such people work much better together than "I" shaped people, who are very good at only one thing. But mostly I always look to employ people much better than me. We get more done. It just works.

Learning 10: Product > Project.

Technology is continually evolving, and the people and processes also need to keep evolving for your business to stay competitive. If you treat transformation as a one-off project, it will most likely result in a painful, expensive failure. You will either run out of budget before you get to your planned end state, or, if by some miracle you do get there, you'll need to immediately start another transformation.

When I was at the MoJ, we had a mantra *"Products not Projects"*. I believe it is much safer to treat transformation as an ongoing product that keeps adapting to meet the needs of your customers and your business.

Transformation is something every business needs to be good at. It is something every CIO should be good at, too. It is the new normal.

About Chris Michael

Chris Michael has been at the forefront of technology for over 30 years, building high performing teams, platforms and products. He has managed multi-million pound budgets and generated hundreds of millions of pounds revenue and profit for global blue-chip brands, across many sectors. Chris is an Agile evangelist, who knows how to get value from data. He has a passion for public cloud and open source tech, and in his spare time advises and mentors start-ups on digital technology.

Chris is currently Head of Technology at *Open Banking*, where he is leading a number of teams to design the API standards for banking in the UK. He is also building an open source banking platform called *Ozone*, and helping his son launch a comedy mobile app called *Laughs*.

https://uk.linkedin.com/in/cjemichael

@cjemichael

CIO Challenges

Surviving a digital explosion

Yiannis Levantis

Time travel

I have always been infatuated with technology and the possibilities it opens-up. I started reading computer magazines (and with great interest, the programming code published in them), years before getting a PC (sad but true). It all came to fruition a few years later, when I convinced my father's friend, who had a PC wholesale business, to give me one of his PCs in exchange for a customer application I wrote for him (not so sad anymore).

I've always had great expectations of technology, thinking of what at the time seemed like Sci-Fi scenarios, but even I never expected to experience time travel in my lifetime. Yet, here I am, back in the late 70's/early 80's, where everyone is raving on about this great new thing called *"digital"*. It feels like I'm back at my cousin's room where he was bragging about his first digital *Casio* watch, while I was staring at my now lame-looking *Swatch*.

The world is exploding with technology and I am (for the most part) delighted for it. Yet, in an industry hungry for buzzwords and in-part promotive of the confusion they carry, I feel I am not alone in being unclear about the term digital and what people think or understand when using it.

In the last two or three years, I have seen anything from a simple, non-transactional website, to a robotics and *IoT* factory setup being referenced under the banner *"digital".* While from a dictionary standpoint, that is all accurate, surely, the relatively recent explosion of the term does not refer to the basic definition of digital computing that has been around for decades.

Today's business executives are under constant pressure to think of new business models and *"be digital".* CIOs are constantly bombarded with terms and trends that few fully understand and while trying to make sense of it all, they're wondering if they should change their title to CDO or risk being perceived as purely operational, unimaginative or even irrelevant.

What is Digital?

So, what is Digital and how do you get hold of and keep a seat at the front of the change?

I have asked the question many times and done a fair amount of research. I have not managed to get to a single, complete and clear definition. Some think of customer-facing technologies which act as, direct and indirect, sales and marketing channels. Others think of technological advancements like *Big Data, Cloud, Machine Learning* and *IoT.*

I'd like to attempt to give my perspective and clarify.

Digital is (very) old news. The first digital computer dates back in the 40's (that's 1940's for the millennials reading this). The first, home-use, mass-marketed PCs date back to the late 70's and early 80's. The digitisation of music with MP3s became available for mass use in the mid-90's and the *iPhone* is 10 years old.

So, what is all the hype about?

It's all about the data

Historically, creation of data has been relatively slow, with limited ways in which to do it. Further, the storage, processing and exchange of data has been expensive and therefore limited to what has been perceived to be the most valuable data. Finally, the analysis of large datasets, and especially unstructured data (see, *Facebook* post after a long, Saturday night pub visit) have been particularly challenging to make sense of and therefore get value from.

However, in recent years, all three of these limitations have been rapidly disappearing. Creation of data has exploded, with mass access to PCs, sensors and *IoT* devices, mobile devices, wearables and the platforms that make it compelling to share it. The cost of storage and computing power has been aggressively decreasing – three decades ago, a terabyte of storage would cost upward of a million dollars, while today it's immediately available, at mass, online or in physical format, for well under a hundred. Finally, Artificial Intelligence and Machine Learning technologies have been advancing significantly, making the deciphering of mass, structured and unstructured data possible.

As data creation is exploding and storage, analysis and transfer are becoming increasingly cheaper and easier, consumption is similarly exploding. Some for personal interactions (sure, we can call it social if you insist), personal use (automation of daily tasks, home automation etc.) and for business value (improved and wider consumer reach, operational improvement and cost reduction, new business models etc.)

It is true that the present and the future are exciting and full of opportunity. However, the mix of technology explosion and hunger for new revenue streams have led to a plethora of misunderstood terms and buzzwords, confusion in leadership roles (CIO, CDO, CTO, Digital Entrepreneur, Digital Strategy

Consultant, should I go on…?) and an increasing challenge in managing the change to generate business success.

Surviving the explosion and thriving on the shockwave

I will not bore you with any technical views as to how and when to use what technology. Instead, I'd like to suggest three key principles for making sense of it all and staying on top and in the driving seat.

1. Keep it simple, real and relevant

While the technology landscape is increasing in complexity (and opportunity), the main principles around its use and value remain broadly the same. Creation, storage and consumption of data for the purposes of automation and business improvement.

Thought, vision and discussion should start and be based on simple, well understood ideas regarding what it is that needs to be achieved, rather than be driven by trendy technological terms that may or may not be relevant or immediately feasible. For example, a conversation about manufacturing automation, quality improvement, cost reduction, preventive maintenance and minimum downtime is one that everyone will be able to follow and visualise. Drive the same conversation though with sensors, IoT, Big Data and Data Lakes, Machine Learning and Advanced Data Analytics and you are bound to confuse yourself and everyone around you.

The means are not to be mixed with the end. I'm pretty sure that Uber wasn't born out of a conversation about Google APIs, mobile-first strategy and electronic payments but from one around resource availability, convenience, immediacy and cost.

2. Avoid the temptation of buzzword-bingo and educate

We all find ourselves having to stay current with the latest technologies and terms. What they really mean, how attainable they are today, what opportunities they present to our business. Like with previous waves of technological advancement, a new vocabulary of terms is generated.

Rather than fall in the trap of proliferating partially understood or altogether misunderstood technology terms, stay focused on demystifying the buzz. Translate buzzwords to clearly defined and understood concepts, giving parallels to existing, well-understood ideas.

Cloud infrastructure is not an ethereal entity, it is simply someone else's datacentres. Virtualised and made resilient in very similar ways that your *"own/on-premise"* datacentre is. And by the way, your *"on-premise"* datacentre, is probably someone else's datacentre anyway.

XaaS (IaaS, PaaS, SaaS etc.) are not magical ways of accessing hardware and software. It is a consumption-based charging model for infrastructure, application development/deployment platforms and the applications themselves (although some software vendors insist on destroying this value with multi-year lock-in periods).

Yes, of course there are peculiarities that come with these. Cloud infrastructure needs to be dealt with differently from a management, security and application development/ deployment perspective. *SaaS* does introduce limitations as to how much you customise the applications, which can be seen as a good or a bad thing. But don't let these peculiarities confuse a concept which is simple to understand and a commercial model (shared resources charged on a consumption basis) that has been around for ever.

And one last thing. Your five-year-old ERP system, your 12 CRM systems, the well-working but very aged master data management database you use, the spaghetti-junction of a BI setup you deliver reports with; all digital. Digital doesn't always mean new and sexy. Ignore the core technologies your business lives on and risk building a load of non-integrated, soon-to-be irrelevant (but lovely looking!) "digital" solutions.

3. Clear Leadership

With the introduction of new technologies, unsurprisingly, there has been a similar increase in new job titles, many of which revolve around the term *"digital"*. And as if the increasing complexity and confusion around emerging technologies was not enough to grapple with, confusion around technology leadership is starting to creep in.

Marketing agencies that use websites and mobile apps as marketing tools are now calling themselves digital agencies. Digital Strategy consultants are knocking on your door daily. Companies are wondering whether they should recruit a Chief Digital Officer and whether he/she should report to the CIO or the CEO. In the meantime, the CIO is left scratching his head, wondering which part of his job is not digital.

At times of complexity, confusion and opportunity, clear, strong, accountable leadership is needed more than ever. The increasing number of technologies, their growing relevance to our business and the pressure to employ them effectively should not be translated into multiple roles of technology leadership. It is unlikely the introduction of additional instruments to an orchestra would call for a second and third orchestra conductor.

What is required is not a segregation of leadership but an adjusted style and capability. It was long ago that technology leaders moved away from the black-box IT operation. They had to develop into much more socially, commercially and business astute leaders, that understood their business, developed deep and wide business process expertise and could be effective negotiators of multi-million software, hardware and services deals, in order to effectively support the business they worked for.

Today, where on several occasions technology is becoming the business itself, or at least is becoming inextricably linked to business success, the technology leader is not there just to support. He/she needs to be an imaginative business idea generator, able to collaborate on or lead the creation of new business models and revenue streams. That said, this should not be misunderstood for an excuse to let technical expertise wither. Deep technical understanding is becoming more critical in managing the multiple fronts of innovation.

Similarly, the business executive of today, cannot any longer go by with a superficial understanding of technology. They must have (or dig deep and find) a genuine interest for technology. They have to pursue technology knowledge that until not long ago would seem unnecessary.

Job titles aside, the cross-section of a business executive with extensive technical understanding and a business-astute, creative technology executive is much better equipped to succeed in an age of digital explosion, than the introduction of trendy-sounding titles and leadership segregation that should instead be specialisation under common leadership.

Simpler than it looks (and feels)

Some openly admit it, some don't but I think most of us feel overwhelmed with the amount of change, innovation and new knowledge we need to keep up with. The past few years. non-IT colleagues seem to be taking an exceptional interest in technology. Which on the one hand is great news (friends! at last!) but add to that occasionally partial knowledge, buzzword confusion and a keen interest to be the next "digital" leader and you may end up with a bit of a challenge.

Although at times it doesn't feel like it, it is possible to be in control and be highly successful, without missing out on the latest technology trends. Resist the temptation to proliferate the confusion. Focus yourself and others on simple, sensible business concepts that remain valid independent of technology trends. Be the one that deciphers tech jargon into simple, easy to grasp ideas. Be the architect to bring it all together and get the value out of it. Insist on clear, accountable and current leadership.

As we're all racing to digitise the world, connect everything to everything and commoditise technology, Artificial Intelligence is entering our personal and working lives at breakneck speeds. And while Elon Musk is packing his rucksack for Mars, we may want to pause and think where we are heading. Because soon, for the first time in human history, we will reach the point when advancing to the next level of technological capability will not require any human initiative, intervention or involvement.

But that's probably the subject of a different, longer article…

About Yiannis Levantis

Mr. Yiannis Levantis has most recently been Group CIO at BMI Group, a €3bn revenue and 11K employee manufacturing company. Previous to that he was Global IT Director at *Rolls Royce Plc. Aerospace and Defence*.

Mr Levantis has also held senior technology roles in large corporations such as *Unilever, Johnson & Johnson* and *GlaxoSmithKline* and has extensive, global experience in technology strategy and execution of complex, multi-million/multi-year business transformation programs.

Mr. Levantis has been a non-Executive Director on the Board of *HCi Viocare*[1] (Bio-engineering, Sensors and IoT) since 2015, enabling collaborations with major brands in the automotive, healthcare and sports industries. He is an Associate of the *Institute For the Future* (IFF) [2], University of Nicosia, with a focus on Artificial Intelligence, Blockchain[3] and Virtual & Augmented Reality. He is a Strategic Advisor for *Artificial Intelligence to the Dubai Centre for Risk and Innovation* (DCRI) [4], part of the British University of Dubai.

Mr. Levantis received a BEng Honours and an MSc in Mechanical Engineering from the University of Manchester Institute of Science and Technology (UMIST) and an MSc in Finance from Aston Business School.

https://www.linkedin.com/in/yiannislevantis/

References

1. http://www.hciviocare.com

2. https://www.unic.ac.cy/research/centres-established-through-university/iff

3. https://www.decentralized.com

4. http://www.buid.ac.ae/DCRI

Building Diverse Organisations

Heena Prajapat

Is it me or is it me? Unconscious biases

It is Phase II of the department re-structure and we are on the second day of interviews. The final checks of the room have been made and my colleague and I are now ready for our candidates.

In walks Brandon, a young professional, slightly nervous in his stance with a casual laptop bag crossed over one shoulder wearing comfortable yet sturdy shoes. He has a full head of curls and a friendly smile. Taking a seat, he becomes more relaxed as the interview progresses and even begins to laugh a little (either I am genuinely funny or he is just being polite - either way, great brownie points!). Brandon does an excellent job of impressing us with his approach to answering our questions, he is well spoken and his cool and calm demeanour make him a great fit for our first line on the service desk. I will definitely be putting him forward for a position.

"Bet you will give him a job!" says my colleague confidently when we conclude. I decide not to give too much away at this point. Although I felt Brandon had made a great impression we must make our decision based on a fair review of all the candidates at the end of the day. I keep my poker face for now.

The colleague who had joined me for the interview process

was a long-standing member of the IT Department which I had joined only six months earlier. My move from the Midlands to the South West of England had been a big life-style change and I was still trying to get used to the local dialect. The welcome gift from my new team had been a book called "A Dictionary of Bristle" by Harry Stoke & Vinny Green, which was a Dictionary of Bristolian phrases and terms that was gratefully received as an aid to my survival in my new home. Thanks to this thoughtful gift I no longer felt uneasy when an elder member of my team greeted me with a cheery "Alreet My Lover!" each morning.

Our process is going well and we are now at candidate four; Carl. In walks a very smartly dressed and assertive young man, he walks with confidence and his warm handshake shows his approachability. This was one of those interviews that gave you the additional benefit of insights into how other companies solve the same IT challenges, and Carl certainly kept us engaged. What a great session and an incredibly intelligent and experienced candidate.

Once again my colleague pipes up at the end of the session. "Bet you won't pick him!" What a fascinating comment I think to myself considering we had just witnessed one of the finest interviews of the day. There was definitely something more to this comment but for now I decide to brush it off.

Finally, at 5pm, we sit down with a well-deserved coffee to collate our scores and decide the fate of the interviewed six. When we name the final three my colleague looks stunned. "I knew you would pick Brandon but I am surprised you have gone for Carl".

"Carl was brilliant! Why would you think I wouldn't select Carl?" I ask politely yet curiously. Nothing prepared me for the response that came next.

"Well his strong Bristolian accent of course!" I am not sure who is more shocked, me at the revelation or my colleague at my stunned expression. "When we interviewed for Phase I you picked the only candidate that didn't have a Bristolian accent" he recalled.

I gather my thoughts or rather attempt to maintain a level of calm. My poker face has definitely left the building.

Until now I hadn't come across the term unconscious bias. Had I really allowed my judgement to be clouded by my background, personal experiences or cultural environment? Was it a coincidence? Or had my colleagues' unconscious bias kicked in when he reached his conclusion being a fellow Bristolian? What had just happened? Irrespective of who's bias was on the podium the facts remained that we now both questioned the integrity of how we had scored our candidates. This experience became my moral compass from here on and my determination to become more self-aware only grew.

How can we make sure that we don't let our own unconscious biases sway the way we make decisions about people?

How did I do it?

People often ask me "So how did you build diverse teams across the globe in these challenging environments?" Well, I have to be honest here, I didn't set out with this intention, it happened purely by happy coincidence. My focus was not on being diverse but on trying to understand what had come to pass before me and what I could do differently.

The simplistic definition of diverse is to be different. It was a surprise to me when people said I myself had brought diversity to the table by being different. Naively, different to me meant no longer being tall enough for the school basketball team because I had missed the growing spurt that everyone else had over the summer holidays. So imagine my surprise when I was told that I was different because … I was a woman.

If the truth be told no one had ever said this to me before. I had never felt like I missed an opportunity or was rejected because of my gender and nor did I feel I had gained any unfair advantage because of it. But now this is what the media was telling me, and suddenly I became very aware of my gender; how I was being treated and if this made me feel different.

To SQEP or not to SQEP -
My first step in building diverse teams

During my time working for an organisation that provided services to the *Ministry of Defence* I came across many acronyms.

I was fascinated by one acronym in particular that was used in the Nuclear Industry: *SQEP* or *Suitably Qualified and Experienced Person*. Whilst the term *SQEP* is meant to differentiate between people that are required to hold the necessary professional qualifications and experience to carry out their jobs safely I found it very useful when building teams in general.

The intention was not to insist that all of our team members were *Suitably, Qualified, Experienced Persons* but instead to use the acronym *SQEP* to keep us honest. By using *SQEP* as a framework it became apparent that this was a powerful acronym that changed the way that we recruited, managed and allocated our teams. For example: we now began to ask and understand why, if at all, someone needed to have a particular certification to do the job (Q = to be qualified) or have relevant industry or subject matter expertise to be a good fit for a role (E = to be experienced).

From *"Are you sure you are SQEP to review my technical design?"* through to *"Do you really need to be SQEP in this subject to help us devise our new processes?"* The term soon became a part of everyday debate to unlock my team's decision-making approach to people. There were times when we decided that we needed only *'Experienced'* and not *'Qualified'* people and other times we didn't need either, just somebody with a little common sense who was willing to learn (S = Suitable).

We now began to have very illuminating conversations that led us to the right type of person for the right job versus the obvious choices we might have always made. Thinking differently gave way to very positive results. Dare I say it, we were now on a journey towards diverse thinking which in turn meant building diverse teams.

How do you SQEP? Application of SQEP

So, continuing on from before; once Phase II of the department re-structure and interviewing had successfully concluded, I was at a whole new phase of my own career through a promotion. This brought with it the challenge of working with a larger disparate team made up of people who were of varying ages and from different global locations who brought different values and life experiences to the table.

During my time evaluating IT functions to establish what a better performing team might look like, I came across North and South divides, competitiveness between floors within the same building and even wariness of colleagues who worked in different departments. Sound familiar?

In order to move away from the natural tendency to gravitate towards familiarity, territory, specialism or location and towards a more fit-for-purpose function, we needed to think outside of the box. Yet again SQEP came to the rescue. By using the acronym to challenge our thinking we had stopped focussing on geographies, sites and obvious candidates for promotion as the primary focus. We started to discover people who were experienced but quieter (E), qualified but in a different country (Q) and more suitable but currently in a different role (S). This gave way to a fresh new structure that was filled with the right people for the right job.

During any department restructure or transformation journey it can be quite difficult to motivate a team and gain their trust that you are here to help when the consensus is otherwise.

There can be a fear amongst the team that asks the question "Will you build a new team by replacing us? Optimise the team by up-skilling us? Or will you just take what might be seen as the easy route and just outsource all of us?" Once again, using *SQEP* helped us to take a closer look at the teams we had, their skills, their experience and but most of all what made them human. An individual's suitability could only fairly be measured by engaging with them, getting to know them and really listening to what they had to say, this was key.

Job descriptions became relaxed and focused more on the person than the skills and team members started to become more self-aware about how *SQEP* they felt they were or needed to be as they applied for roles in the new structure. And guess what? As a by-product of this approach the outcome was a truly diverse team made up of diverse thinking, representation from different sites, locations, ages and gender.

Conclusion

Diversity to me meant recruiting a non-IT person from the business who was more *SQEP* and that understood a business process better than the IT function did. Bringing an Engineer to the IT department was previously seen as a demotion by the Engineering team but a promotion by the IT team. However, the business now felt they had a voice at the table and IT understood the business better ... Win/Win

Diversity to me meant discovering who it was that wrote that punchy, clear and concise paragraph in the network performance section of the monthly report, clearly a very *SQEP* team member. Asking the author to step forward and come to the management meetings in person revealed that Donna (the author) was in fact the glue to the network team. The silent gear that had never dared raise her head above the parapet was now given a voice and coached to be more confident. She later became the Network Manager.

In my experience, diversity begins with:

- Being diverse of thought and being aware of any unconscious bias you may be acting out and then parking it to one side.
- Taking more time to listen, be present and observe so that you can better understand what is in front of you.
- Engaging with and seeking out diverse thinking from all levels of the organisation, nurturing this thinking and giving it a voice.
- Using the acronym SQEP as a tool to challenge your thinking and approach to recruiting, managing and allocating teams.

In addition, before launching into deciphering the 'How do we build diverse teams?' conundrum I have learnt to remind myself that each environment will have its own story to tell and it is important to take time to listen to it through the people and remain curious while doing so.

To summarise, unconscious bias is present in all of us because of our experiences in life and this is normal. The secret is to notice it in ourselves, park it to one side, and to use tools and techniques around you which can help you look at things from a different angle to work successfully for the benefit of the business, team and yourself.

Diversity ultimately starts with you.

About Heena Prajapat

Heena Prajapat is an IT Transformation specialist. Heena has over 17 years of experience with a passion for technology and how it can bring efficiency, innovation and business benefit to an organisation.

Heena has worked in diverse and complex global organisations with large teams all over the world bringing a wealth of experience with many different cultures.

Heena's career to date has a running theme of "IT Transformation" throughout and her journey has taken her from strategic IT change initiatives at G4S through to global programme delivery to deliver stability and drive innovation at *Rolls-Royce*.

Heena started in IT Service Delivery and then progressed in to IT leadership positions including Group IT Manager, Head of IT and Head of Technology Solutions & Support. Her experience spans the *Defence, Marine and Aerospace Industries* in global organisations.

https://www.linkedin.com/in/heena-prajapat01/

Building your own capability for transformation through the senior Gig Economy

Pat Lynes

CIOs have never been in a better position to step forward and own the business transformation now that all organisations are technology based. This gives the CIO the opportunity to be right at the heart of the board agenda.

I've been designing and deploying technology, change and leadership capability for over 15 yeas and have delivered over 100 transformations for CIOs and change agents for companies of all sizes that include *Burberry, Mastercard/ Vocalink* and *BskyB*. In recognition of my contribution to industry, I was awarded *Global Interim Recruiter of the Year* in 2015 by a major industry body.

This chapter is my take on what you can do to make sure you have the capability to transform your organisations and your career. I have shared some techniques I use to help CIOs deliver certainty in an uncertain world.

Upon my travels in my former life as an Interim recruiter who built capability for CIOs, and now as Founder of *Sullivan & Stanley – The Change Society*, I've spoken to many CIOs and other change agents about the problems that they face as executives. There are three that kept cropping up time and time again.

Capability Gap

CIOs don't have the people they need and the leadership capability they need to facilitate change.

Speed Gap

CIOs are in organisations that haven't the ability nor agility to change. They are hamstrung as the organisational design is a 20th Century one and not fit for the 21st Century. Augment that with significant technical debt and you can see why so many organisations have declining revenues.

Current routes to capability are failing and outdated (via the use of out of touch recruiters, advisory and management consultancy models)

The ultimate problem is that large organisations stifled with enormous waste, bureaucracy and the complexity of emergent change may not exist in the next decade if they don't put change at the heart of the agenda and develop that capability muscle.

This is quite the responsibility on today's CIO to own the business transformation whilst driving new operating models and still operating BAU.

The traditional enterprise model of outsourcing your strategy and technology problems to external providers has created a legacy of slow moving organisations with hardly any learning culture which isn't suited to the modern pace of today's technological change or modern workforce.

Newer, more agile and responsive disruptive businesses are fast eating corporate market share and it is now imperative for CIOs to have their own change capability, but some are woefully underprepared.

Organisations and CIOs must prepare organisations for constant change and here is my take on how you could look to close this capability and speed gap

Different ways of working are unfolding amid an economic climate of uncertainty and constant change. Year on year, the rate of technological advancement increases and day by day, the capability and speed gaps widen whilst the war for premium talent and skill rages on.

Today, more than ever before, organisations need to be agile and capable of delivering change and innovation at pace. If CIOs are to meet board expectations, optimising technology operations and owning the innovation agenda, then new ways of augmenting capability need to be explored.

But the rapidly widening capability gap makes meeting these imperatives difficult. These complex organisational challenges are demanding that CIOs and organisations think differently and consider new, relevant practices, rather than hold on to past practices that are failing to deliver.

Such seismic changes require a completely different mind-set and different partnership model, where value, agility and sustainability are prioritised. The simple fact is that within a constantly changing climate, methods that used to work, no longer do.

Where the 20th Century corporation focused on efficient production using labour and capital, the 21st Century corporation co-creates and innovates at pace using knowledge networks and a fusion of entrepreneurship and intrapreneurship.

We know for sure the old world is dying and the new world is happening. The collision of these worlds is causing chaos and complexity making change increasingly hard to facilitate and deliver. Indeed, for some, change is too rapid to know where to even start the transformation.

Many find it hard balancing today's demands keeping the estate running whilst delivering tomorrow's essentials along with the constant pressure from the board to innovate.

CIOs have boards to address, and the boards have shareholders to keep happy whilst also maintaining personal ambition, bonus payments and safeguarding the certainly of a good career. Add to this the fear of failing and it creates the drive for some to outsource the problem to the usual partners.

But there is a booming workforce out there ready to be deployed on demand through what I call the *Executive and Knowledge Gig Economy.*

The Booming Executive and Knowledge Gig Economy

Talented people have discovered that creating a flexible, work-life balance is no longer a pipe dream. I have personally interviewed thousands of senior knowledge workers and executives within technology and change and the prevalent message is that many are done with corporate politics and are deciding to vote with their feet and head into the Gig Economy to have a different relationship with their career and start a portfolio of opportunities.

They can maximise and optimise their output, income and strengths in exchange for autonomy, choice in work and a more balanced working life.

This is what I call the *Executive and Knowledge Gig Economy* – where companies contracting independent workers for engagements is increasingly commonplace; an evolution of the trend away from a job for life towards multiple job changes that create a more rewarding journey.

I've personally seen a significant rise in the number of highly skilled, strategic thought-leaders, knowledge workers and change agents entering Interim management and the freelance senior *"gig world."*

CIOs should be aware of this extensive network of agile talent and leadership that can be deployed into the business through the right trusted partners like *Sullivan & Stanley*.

The rise of this *Executive* or *Knowledge Gig Economy* has empowered workers to concentrate on journeys rather than jobs where the experience and freedom is more coveted than the security of a permanent job or career path.

The future knowledge worker is demanding flexibility and the Top 5% of talent are voting with their feet. The permanent to gigster way of working is increasing.

There's a huge opportunity for businesses here, and a large pool of flexible, highly skilled workers, leaders and change agents to tap into on-demand. CIOs, change agents and the rest of the C-Suite have a real opportunity to utilise a scalable workforce that can help them meet the needs of their business agenda and close the ever-growing capability and speed gap.

The sooner CIOs and organisations embrace this way of working (as an enabler, rather than a cost), the more empowered they will be in the future as the competition for Top 5% resource becomes even fiercer.

A recent Deloitte report, *The Open Talent Economy*, explains:

"The evolving workforce is a mixture of employees, contractors and freelancers, and – increasingly – people with no formal ties to the enterprise at all.

Deloitte defines open talent as a collaborative, transparent, technology-enabled, rapid-cycle way of doing business. What the opensource model did for software, the open talent economy is doing for work, the report says, concluding, "in this new economy, access to talent is more important than ownership of talent".

So how do CIOs capitalise on this shift to solve, deliver and thrive in the next decade?

My solution is to shift towards crowdsourcing project-based work, rather than relying on searching for a compliment of full-time employees or outsourcing the problem; to hire teams and tap into knowledge networks that can be harnessed to crowd around specific problems; and deliver desired outcomes, whilst also upskilling your core permanent team, rather than outsource and lose control, learnings and IP.

Outsourcing, offshoring and onshoring for knowledge work has failed to reduce the capability gap or win the war for talent, so crowdsourcing within this *Executive and Knowledge Gig Economy* has become a fresher and more valuable alternative.

Traditional recruitment models put the CIOs organisations under extensive interview debt and outsourcing to management consulting firms hasn't been the silver bullet either.

Both traditional routes to capability have cost millions in forecasted and hidden costs, and neither has left organisations with a sustainable capability. Often, it has given the higher quality permanent people cause to leave.

With crowdsourcing, you can leverage the Gig Economy to source solutions from the best minds in the world within a tailored talent pool like our *Change Society*. CIOs can now reach out to the crowd to co-create solutions that work and help develop their core permanent team.

My four rapid actions points for CIOs who would like to trial crowdsourcing the Gig Economy

1. Put Top 5% Interim Talent into your strategy

The best talent is far more productive than the rest, but most CIOs and organisations do not plan pro-actively to secure the best talent and/or leaders. To be fair, most have internal processes and suppliers they are bound to use by HR and procurement.

Look for fresh alternatives and suppliers that have access to Top 5% talent as the best can do more at a faster pace and do it better.

CIOs need to look at implementing new sourcing models to achieve more at less cost. That's why I'm a big advocate of hiring three or four elite people rather than ten or fifteen average people at more cost. The best will inevitably save you time, energy and money.

CIOs can now work with partners such as *Sullivan & Stanley* to anticipate their needs and orchestrate skills and expertise to help solve the capability and skills gap issue.

2. Outcome and Statement of Work based teams

I believe that Interims are one of the most underused and underrated routes to capability in the market. They tend to over deliver, are loyal to you and want to make maximum impact in a short space of time as they know they are only as good as their last gig. Take this a step further and look at deploying teams of Top 5% Interims and you can achieve massive results at a rapid pace.

3. Experiment with the *"Teams as a Service"* approach to delivering projects and change

The *Teams as a Service (TaaS)* model involves hiring, through a trusted partner, a team of Interims. An agile talent collective; to crowdsource around any problem and/or opportunity to deliver key objectives and outcomes. CIOs should start to experiment with new models like this to solve their capability and speed gap issues. These teams can be cross-pollinated with your permanent capability to make sure learning, knowledge and IP is left in the business.

When you crowdsource Top 5% it gives you an emergent, vibrant network of people to call upon who are *"can-do"*, solution centric types that you need in any organisation. Experiment with putting problems out to a crowd of people who have got the experience and want you to be a success.

4. Create all-star cross functional teams to tackle CIOs highest priority issues

Teaming great talent in a cross functional way not only acts as a force multiplier but also helps align business and technology to deliver quickly. Creating blended teams that are mission focused creates an environment where the cross-pollination of ideas and entrepreneurial thinking is encouraged.

We have had great success working with CIOs by helping them deploy mission based teams that can operate with their sponsorship away from the bureaucracy and over processed organisation they sit in through the *Teams as a Service* model.

Summary

CIOs can future-proof their careers and organisation by having an agile response to change. One which taps into the collective minds of smaller, focused hand-picked teams.

These teams can crowd-source around your problems and help you deliver the business transformation in iterations.

I believe the old method of relying on the traditional top four consultancies is starting to change and as we enter this *VUCA* (volatile, uncertain, complex, ambiguous) world. I believe there is a great opportunity for CIOs to experiment and trial other routes to capability that can encourage learning, sharing and most of all deliver success throughout their organisations. The Gig Economy gives them access to Top 5% people to help them close the capability and speed gap forever.

About Pat Lynes

Pat Lynes has been at the top of the  IT and change knowledge worker recruitment game for over 15 years and was *Global Interim Recruiter of the Year, 2015.*

He has successfully delivered over 100 transformation teams for the likes of *Burberry, Argos, Sky* and *Everything Everywhere.*

Pat was part of the leadership team that won *Best Company To Work For* and *Fastest Growing Company* in the UK for five consecutive years.

He delivered a seven figure divisional business for a large global technology recruitment company and also recently co-built the largest independent technology and change recruitment company in the UK to an eight figure revenue business within six years.

Visioning a future world for his game he decided to create the challenger brand, *Sullivan & Stanley,* to solve CIO and board problems around the widening *capability* and *speed* gap in today's organisations.

Sullivan & Stanley is a premiere top 5% crowd company for executive Interims, the originator of the *Teams as a Service* model and the *Change Society* professional community designed to transform and future-proof companies against disruptive technology.

Pat is married to Helen, with two boys, Sullivan and Stanley.

www.sullivanstanley.com

https://www.linkedin.com/in/patricklynes/

pat.lynes@sullivanstanley.com

@patlynes

Our Tech Skills Time Bomb

Abby Ewen

I was asked recently what I thought the biggest challenge facing the CIO was in the next five years. I considered the obvious issues like moving from a *capex* to an *opex* model, the impact of artificial intelligence, the exponential demands of customers, and the continuing demands to provide more for less. However, my answer was that I thought it lay in the very significant skills and capability gap I see looming for all of us. A number of CIOs have echoed this in recent weeks, noting that it is already becoming harder to recruit good people with the right skills in timescales to suit their business objectives.

The *2016 Hays Global Skills Index* found that Britain's skills shortage had worsened for the fifth consecutive year. The survey suggested that university degrees do not provide either the technical nor vocational knowledge required by businesses. It concluded that the skills gap has worsened by 8% over the past five years.

A recent survey of small firms by a private equity firm noted that the UK education system is more of an obstacle for high growth companies in filling jobs than the uncertainty surrounding *Brexit*.

More than 1.5m people already work in the UK digital sector or in digital roles across other sectors and the digital sector is growing at a rate twice as fast as non-digital sectors.

The UK has been described as 'the digital capital of Europe'- with higher degrees of investment in digital tech than any other country in Europe. If we hold back growth in the tech sector, we run the risk of holding back growth of the whole UK economy.

My sense is that over the next five to ten years, this gap is going to grow, and there are a number of reasons for this.

Mind the Education Gap

Firstly, whilst we may be surrounded by millennials who are *'digital natives'* and who are extremely comfortable and confident in their use of technology, it seems that many of them are less interested in how the technology works, or in taking up roles in the technology industry.

Rapid and exponential changes in consumer technology and the impact of social media may also be contributing to that capability gap.

The traditional education system is unfortunately a little disadvantaged in this respect. As more and more schools phase out courses and qualifications in the more creative elements of technology, fewer children are getting engaged with it. Whilst it is commendable that the new national curriculum requires pupils to learn *Python* scripting, not all technology roles require the ability to code. In fact, channelling pupils down this route may have the negative effect of turning them off to technology.

Unsurprisingly, careers advisers in secondary schools are not equipped to assist pupils with advice on careers in technology. In a world where jobs types are disappearing, and new ones appearing in their place, this is a voyage into the unknown for most pupils, teachers and careers counsellors.

There are not enough people in schools with a passion for and understanding of technology in the real world to be able to evangelise and really spark that interest and enthusiasm which is needed to pursue a career in technology or even understand what roles may be available and what skills are needed for those roles.

STEM Cells

Some of these gaps can be filled by *STEM Ambassadors*, a network of volunteers backed up by a database of ambassador opportunities to match to the volunteers.

One of the observations I have made is that educational establishments make the mistake of pitching technology as a *'thing'* or an entity when the reality is that it is a ubiquitous part of life which weaves itself into the fabric of everything around us.

Having carried out mentoring opportunities at a number of different schools over the past couple of years it is clear to see that when children and young adults are asked to think about technology in the right way the innovative ideas they have are impressive and unbounded.

One group of girls I worked with recently thought that *'Wi-Fears'* were a great invention - Wi-Fi hotspots inside your earrings. Children have not yet been conditioned to consider things like their market demographics, manufacturing costs, distribution challenges etc. They use their imaginations in an unconstrained way, but for many reasons this is then not translating into enough of an interest in a career in IT. Whilst this is a problem across both sexes, it is particularly prevalent when it comes to encouraging girls to take up tech careers. There are so many stereotypes surrounding careers in the digital world, and very few of these stereotypes appeal to teenage girls. STEM ambassadors can be crucial here too, helping to break down some of these stereotypes and demonstrating the vast range of interesting roles and the skills and qualifications required to fill them.

Bridging that Gap

One of the positive potential counters to these challenges is the growth of UTCs or University Technical Colleges. Industry backed, and aimed at 14-19 year olds, they are designed to provide innovative education combining technical, practical and academic learning. UTCs have a special focus on science, technology, engineering and maths subjects and are very much based on 'outcomes' rather than GCSE or A-Level pass rates.

I have met very impressive young people emerging from these colleges who are already better equipped to understand the practical elements of the world of work. One has founded his own artificial intelligence tech start-up at the age of 19. Alongside the traditional academic subjects of Maths and English, students can specialise in subjects that engage them and are provided with opportunities to work with employer partners in real working environments. Despite their vocational nature, however, figures just released for 2016 UTC leavers note that 44% of leavers went to university, (compared to 28.1% nationally). 29% of leavers started an apprenticeship (compared to 8.4% nationally). Of all UTC leavers, only 0.5% ended up not in education, employment or training, which is significantly below the national average.

We need advanced technical skills in order to create a prosperous future, and our education system, both secondary and tertiary, needs to reflect the modern world of work and allow us to nurture our home-grown talent.

Brexit Brain Drain

This leads to the second issue. Part of the solution to our home-grown skills shortage is to encourage skilled immigrants, and the UK has always relied on foreign labour.

Unfortunately, since the UK's vote to leave the EU, the number of foreign candidates in the UK candidate pool has fallen by 50%. Allied to this, there also appears to be a growing trend amongst UK companies to employ fewer foreign workers.

This triple whammy of fewer immigrants to fill roles, a home-grown workforce who are not being encouraged into digital jobs and the growth of the digital sector suggests that the skills shortage may present us with a very serious challenge.

There are new jobs yet to be discovered, and old jobs disappearing, but they require most of the same skills – lateral thinking, problem solving, people management, and analytical skills. This may lead us into a further potential challenge.

Seeing the Light

There is no doubt that technology has changed the human race profoundly. Medical breakthroughs to save lives happen every day. We can land probes on meteors, grow skin, understand how the universe began, map DNA, and obviously post selfies at 3 o'clock in the morning.

There is a new alternative branch of science understanding the medium and long-term impact on lifeforms of the constant availability of light. When we all lived in caves we got up when it was light and we went to bed when it was dark, with our bodies working to the circadian rhythm where we would get more sleep in the winter and less in the summer. All of our rhythms are now broken. It is potentially light all the time in the developed world and we go to bed with our tablets, phones and laptops.

This reduced exposure to sunlight and increased exposure to electrical light is delaying our internal clocks. This affects our brain because of its neuroplasticity, or its ability to change.

Plastic Fantastic

Research proves that our brains are more plastic when we are young, and that this declines with age. Plasticity happens throughout our lives. It makes the brain resilient and is the process by which permanent learning takes place – learning how to play a musical instrument or speak a different language. But this same characteristic, which makes our brains amazingly resilient, also make them vulnerable to outside and internal, usually unconscious, influences. And our brains have never before been assaulted by so many influences and stimuli.

The brain is quite extraordinary. What actually changes in the brain are the strengths of the connections of neurones that are engaged together, moment by moment, in time. The more something is practiced, the more connections are changed. Initial changes are temporary. The brain first records the change, then determines whether it should make the change permanent or not. It only becomes permanent if the brain judges the experience to be fascinating or novel enough, or if the behavioural outcome is important, good or bad.

However, each time our brains strengthen a connection to advance our mastery of a skill, it also weakens other connections of neurones that weren't used at that precise moment. This negative plastic brain change erases some of the irrelevant or interfering activity in the brain.

Brain plasticity is a two-way street; it is just as easy to generate negative changes as it is positive ones. You have a *"use it or lose it"* brain. It's almost as easy to drive changes that impair memory and physical and mental abilities as it is to improve these things.

The Shallows

To technology and its impact on how we process facts and information. Nicholas Carr is the author of a book called *The Shallows,* the thrust of which is that the Internet is rewiring our brains, inducing only superficial understanding. The plasticity of our brains is what allows this to happen.

This is leading to profound changes in the way we live and communicate, remember and socialise - even in our very conception of ourselves. Are we going to end up with future generations who wouldn't be able to write a dissertation but can multitask with 3 different user interfaces at the same time?

Our brains are also programmed to filter out a lot of inputs. In a world where we are now being bombarded by communications, are our brains adapting to that constant bombardment by becoming superficial? Negative plasticity?

My hope is that the jobs we will be doing in the future are exactly the jobs which our brains are equipping us for.

What impact will that ultimately have on the way that we develop software or implement solutions?

Should we be thinking about employing UX or user interface designers who will create interfaces to appeal to the *'shallow'* people. This is a very different approach to the approach we have currently.

Is this just the natural evolution of the *Human Computer Interface* that we have wrestled with for years? Some of us adapt well to consistent and continuous technological change – it kind of goes with the territory as a CIO. But with all the stimulation and input, is this actually getting harder for all of those who would not call themselves digital natives?

STEMming the Flow

In conclusion, I believe that those of us who have worked in this industry have a duty to get involved in education at every level and at every stage so that we can at least start to resolve the first of these challenges. This may be by backing a UTC from an organisational perspective or by creating structured mentoring programmes to enthuse young people.

We all need to be using the experience we have gathered over our decades in technology roles to encourage future generations and ensure that the UK stays at the forefront of the digital economy.

About Abby Ewen

Abby Ewen has been IT Director at *BLM* for four and a half years. Prior to this she spent 10 years at *Simmons & Simmons* where she was Director of Business Transformation and ten years at *Withers*. Abby is responsible for aligning technology change across the firm in a strategic way, providing technology solutions and innovations for internal and external clients. Abby has a passion for business change and a desire to inspire this passion in others.

Abby has a talent for reengineering roles, reshaping resources to satisfy new initiatives, and has the ability to see how the market is changing and how the business needs to change to be more effective and meet new demands. Technology plays a key part in the success of the firm. She is also a STEM Ambassador and is focused on encouraging school children to take up careers in the exciting and evolving world of technology.

https://www.linkedin.com/in/abby-ewen-6158354/

Join Us.

We would like to invite you to join this growing movement of CIOs/CTOs/CDOs – Business leaders with a technology focus as it grows into a global community.

CIO 2.0 is a social community and series of events within a closed executive network, dedicated to helping the CIO/CTO community move into the next decade.

The Portfolio CIO (Exec Gig Economy) and CIO moving to owning the business transformation are our anchors but we meet and workshop on the many different moves a CIO can make that is relevant for the next decade.

The Social CIO	*The Exec Gig Economy CIO*
The Portfolio CIO	*The Transformational CIO*
The Investor CIO	*The Interim CIO*
The Private Equity CIO	*The Impact CIO*
Beyond CIO	*NED CIO*

To join the network please email *CIO@sullivanstanley.com* or call Pat Lynes on 07866 477944 and/or Christian McMahon on 07775 826808.

For more information go to

http://www.cio20.uk/